Sew Charming

To our mums, Margaret and Heather ...
Women who, in the 1970s, introduced
us to Marimekko, made us bright pink
hotpants and seersucker dresses, and
who were responsible for sewing the
thread ... that lead ... to this
infinite passion!

Sew Charming

40 Simple Sewing and Hand-printing Projects for Home and Family

Cath Derksema & Kirsten Junor

POTTER
CRAFT

Contents

PROJECTS

Introduction

Prints Charming — modern contemporary craft

Craft/ed is a great word — it means it was made by hand, it means it was made for someone special, and that is a wonderful thing. We print and stitch all our designs because we love them and would love to craft with them. This book has been written with "handmade" in mind: we want to introduce you to the Prints Charming world of color and embellishment.

Initially frustrated by the lack of fabrics that we would both like to play with, it got us to thinking … what if? What if we could print them ourselves? So that's what we began to do, back in 2002. We still use the same techniques today and, in the following pages, we explain all the things we do, so you too can get excited by the creative process that is silk-screen printing.

We believe in achievable projects that you can make, use, or share right away. Our approach to the book is "Would we make that, and could we make that at home?" Some of your fabrics you may like to try printing yourself; for others you may think, "I have the perfect fabric for that project in my stash." There are no rules … experiment with color, texture, and scale. Above all, have fun.

We are constantly surprised by the magic of being able to design, print, and sew our own fabrics.

Cath and Kirsten

The basics

Before you begin sewing the projects in this book, here is a list of things you might need and a few terms and techniques that are useful to know, if you don't know already.

Equipment basics

This is a checklist to get you started. If you've ever done any sewing, you'll have many of these things:

❋ **Double-sided fusible web** An adhesive-backed paper that enables you to cut and adhere appliqué shapes to fabric. It also seals the raw edges, to prevent fraying. It is available in fabric or craft stores. Remember that the finished shapes will be mirror-images of the way they were traced — so if you're using letters, you need to trace them back-to-front.

❋ **Dressmaker's chalk** Also known as tailor's chalk. Useful for marking outlines on fabric, it just brushes away when you're finished.

❋ **Dressmaking scissors** Buy the most expensive pair you can afford and only use them for cutting fabric — not paper, or your nails, or

beading wire, or anything else. Threaten the rest of the family if they even look at them!

❋ **Embroidery thread** Our favorite thread is perle cotton No 8, which we use for embroidered embellishment and for most of our quilting (instead of the more traditional, finer, quilting cotton). Perle cotton (sometimes also called "pearl") is a tightly twisted, lustrous, non-divisible thread that comes in a huge range of colors. You can also use stranded embroidery floss — and we sometimes use both.

❋ **Hand-sewing needles** You'll need several sizes for sewing, basting, quilting, and embroidery.

❋ **Iron and ironing board** OK, we know everyone has these tucked away — but remember to set them up when you're sewing and press everything as you go. It makes things much easier and neater.

✳ **Machine needles** These come in a variety of sizes, suitable for sewing a standard fabric, such as cotton or linen, as well as lightweight fabrics, like voile, or heavyweight fabrics, such as denim and canvas. The right needle for your fabric really makes a difference. Machine needles eventually get blunt too — change your needle every so often and you'll be amazed at how much easier it is to sew.

✳ **Paper scissors** These can be those cheap scissors that you get at stationery stores or the supermarket.

✳ **Pins** Essential items for any project involving fabric. Take your pick from standard pins or ones with glass heads.

✳ **Rotary cutter, quilting ruler, and cutting mat** Not absolutely necessary, but really useful for speedy and accurate cutting of patchwork pieces and quilt blocks.

✳ **Seam ripper** Despite the best of intentions, you *will* occasionally make mistakes — this will make them easier to undo!

✳ **Sewing machine** You *could* sew all the projects in this book by hand, but it would take forever and you'd probably get sick of it. We love hand-sewing, but we save it for quilting and embellishing our finished items, or for piecing the odd special quilt. So, you'll probably need a sewing machine. It doesn't need to have a computer and 2,000 embroidery stitches — forwards, backwards, and zigzag is fine. Many of the projects in this book were made using our mums' basic 1970s sewing machines.

✳ **Sewing thread** Use a color to match your project. Buy good-quality thread from a fabric store. Thread from bargain stores is cheaper but also tends to be very inferior.

✳ **Small, sharp scissors** For snipping threads.

✳ **Tape measure** The most useful type is an extra-long one, often used by quilters.

✳ **Tracing paper** Save yourself some time and buy large sheets of dressmakers' tracing paper at fabric stores: much easier for tracing full-size patterns than lots of small sheets that need taping together.

✳ **Zipper foot** A special narrow foot for your sewing machine that allows you to sew close to the edge of the zipper teeth on each side. It usually comes as a standard attachment with most sewing machines.

Sewing basics

This is not an exhaustive list, but when we use these terms in the projects, this is what we mean:

✳ **Baste or tack** Hold pieces together with large hand-stitches until you do the final stitching. You can also machine-baste by choosing the longest stitch available on your machine and stitching in the seam allowance, just outside the seam line.

✳ **Bias** The diagonal of a woven fabric, at a 45-degree angle to the straight grain. Fabric that is cut on the bias will stretch, making it useful for accommodating curves. Bias binding, as the name suggests, is cut on the bias, which means that you can use it to bind around a curved edge.

✳ **Casing** A wide double hem that is used to thread ribbon or elastic through.

✳ **Clip the curves** When you sew a seam around a curve, you need to snip the seam allowance before you turn the item right side out, so that the curved seam will sit nice and flat, without puckers. On convex curves, make a small notch into the seam allowance; on concave curves, simply snip across the allowance towards the seam. In either case, take care not to actually snip into the stitching itself. Make these notches and snips at $1/2$–$3/4$-inch intervals, or even closer on tight curves and around complex shapes.

✳ **Double hem** Turn the raw edge of your fabric to the wrong side — an iron is handy for doing this — then turn under the folded edge again and stitch along the inner edge. This creates a neat hem that completely encloses the raw edge.

✳ **Fat quarter** A piece of fabric that is made by cutting one yard of fabric in halves, first vertically, then horizontally. The piece thus cut is approximately 18 × 22 inches (or 50 × 56 centimeters in metric systems). A fat quarter is still a quarter of a yard, but is in a more user-friendly squarish ("fat") shape, that is more useful for projects than a narrow strip.

✳ **Press under** This means to turn down the raw edge on a piece of fabric, folding wrong sides together, and press with your iron.

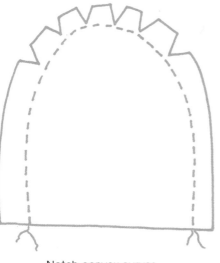

Notch convex curves

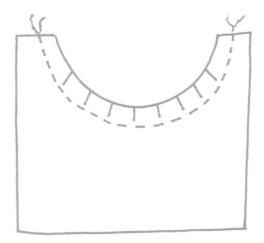

Clip into concave curves

✳ **Right sides together** Place your pieces together so that the outside or patterned sides are facing inwards toward each other, and the wrong sides are facing out.

✳ **Seam allowance** The measurement that you need to add to the edges of your fabric when cutting, to allow for stitching the seams. It can vary from $1/4$ inch to $3/4$ inch, depending on the fabric itself and the nature of your project.

✳ **Selvages** The woven finished edges along the length of a piece of fabric. This woven edge should normally be cut off your fabric before you use it, because it can shrink at a different rate to the rest of the fabric. But don't throw it away! We love selvages and use them as a slightly quirky trim on lots of projects. There are big bags of collected selvages at the studio, waiting to be used!

✳ **Slip stitch** This is a "hidden" stitch, used for hemming and closing openings, for example, after stuffing a pillow. The fabric edge is folded, giving you somewhere to hide your stitches. Knot your thread and bring the needle out through the crease of the fold. Pick up a thread or two of the opposite fabric, push the needle directly back into the fold of the fabric, and push it along the fold before bringing it out a little way further along and picking up another two threads.

✳ **Straight grain** The direction of the weave of a fabric, along either the warp (vertical thread) or the weft (horizontal threads). Pattern pieces cut on the straight grain of a fabric do not stretch. (Compare with Bias.)

✳ **Topstitch** A line of machine-stitching done on the right side of the fabric. It can be used both decoratively and also to add strength to seams and edges.

✳ **Trim the corner** When you sew around a 90-degree corner, such as on a cushion cover, before turning the piece right side out, trim diagonally across each corner, close to the stitching. This reduces the bulk of fabric in the corner so that when you turn the piece right side out, your corners form neat points.

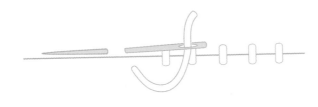

Slip stitch

Quilting basics

This is by no means a comprehensive quilting course, but there are a few standard steps in the making of a quilt that need explaining:

✳ **Layering the quilt** When you have finished constructing your quilt top (always a triumphant moment!), you need to assemble all the layers into a "sandwich." The backing and batting should always be about 4 inches larger all round than the quilt top. Lay your backing piece, right side down, on a flat, clean surface and smooth it out carefully. For extra stability, you can tape the edges down temporarily, using masking tape. Place the batting on top of the backing and smooth it out. On top of the batting, place the well-pressed quilt top, right side up, making sure the top and backing are square to each other. Smooth out any creases.

✳ **Basting layers together** You now need to hold the three layers firmly together for quilting. You can do this by pinning through all three layers with safety pins, at about 8-inch intervals. You can also hand-baste the layers together with a grid of large basting stitches, starting at the center and working out, both horizontally and vertically, at intervals of about 6 inches.

✳ **Quilting** It's very easy to get hung up about quilting, but it's basically just running stitch, worked through all three layers of the quilt to keep them together. If you're going to enter your quilt in a competition, the Stitch Police will want you to quilt it with tiny, even, fairy stitches in a breathtakingly intricate pattern. But if, like us, you just want to hold the layers together in a practical and pleasing way, relax. Instead of quilting thread, we use perle cotton to quilt because it is more visible, the stitches are larger, and results happen faster! If you want to stretch your quilt in a hoop while you work, then go right ahead. Thread a crewel embroidery needle with a length of perle cotton No 8 and make a series of small stitches in and out of the layers of your quilt, following the seam lines, or around printed motifs, or in your chosen design. Hide your starting knot by tugging it sharply so that it "pops" through the top fabric into the batting, where it is concealed.

✳ **Outline-quilting** This means to quilt around the shape of a block or motif, inside or outside the seam or design, matching its outline.

✳ **In-the-ditch quilting** The term that is used for quilting along the seam line. It should be done on the "low" side of the seam, that is, on the side without seam allowance, so you are quilting through three layers of fabric, not five.

✳ **Machine-quilting** Instead of hand-quilting, you may want to machine-quilt your quilt yourself and, on small projects, this is not too difficult. But on anything larger, we use and recommend a professional quilting service because the results are vastly superior to anything we could produce on a home sewing machine. Ask your fabric or quilting store for recommendations.

✳ **Binding** When all quilting is finished, remove basting and trim edges of batting and backing even with quilt top. We use straight edge double-fold binding, as it is easiest and strongest. Measure two opposing sides of your quilt and cut two lengths of binding strip, 2 inches longer than each measured side. Press these lengths in half, wrong sides together. Position raw edges of binding so that they are 1/2 inch from the edge of the quilt and pin in place along the 1/4-inch seam line. Sew binding to quilt. Fold binding over to back of quilt and slip stitch folded edge in place over the stitching line. Trim ends of binding even with edges of quilt. Now bind remaining edges of quilt in the same way, leaving 2 inches extra binding at each end. Sew binding in place, as before, then trim the overhang to 1/2 inch. Fold binding to back and slip stitch as before, neatly tucking in raw ends, and slip stitching folded edges together at corners.

Stitch guide

These are our favorite embroidery stitches that we use over and over and with them you can transform a plain or printed piece of fabric.

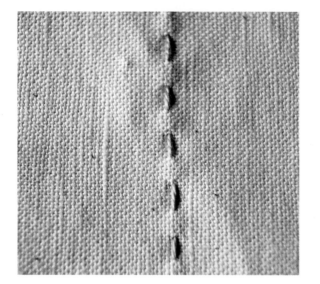

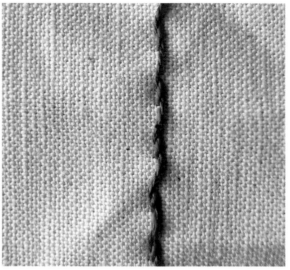

Running stitch We call this the "up and down stitch" and use it all the time. It can be worked along a line that is straight or curved, and it is as simple as guiding your needle up and down through the fabric, keeping the stitches fairly equal in length. Running stitch, worked row after row, can create a great effect and it's so easy!

Whipped running stitch This combination of color and stitches creates a twisted cord effect. After working running stitch in one color, thread a blunt-end tapestry needle in another color. Bring needle up from back to front of fabric, close to the start of running stitch. Take needle under first running stitch (without piercing fabric) from top to bottom and continue to do this with every subsequent running stitch, always working second thread from the same direction.

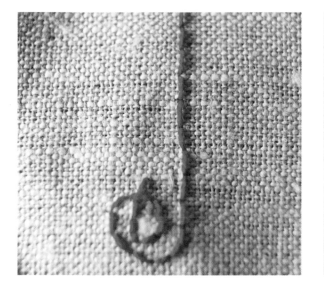

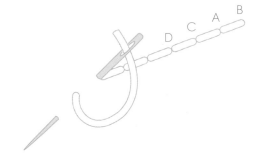

Back stitch This simple stitch makes a great outline and, combined with other stitches, is another favorite of ours. As the name suggests, you bring the needle up and then go "back." Bring the needle to the front at A, take a small stitch backwards, and re-insert it at B. Bring it to the front again at C, take it backwards to A, and so on. Continue to work in this way, creating an unbroken line of stitching.

Blanket and buttonhole stitch These stitches are worked in the same manner — buttonhole stitch is simply a close version of blanket stitch. They can be used to outline a design or edge a fabric piece. Insert the needle from front to back at A, bringing it out again at B, and keeping the thread under the needle point. Pull up the stitch to form a loop. Work the next stitch as close or as far apart from the first stitch as desired.

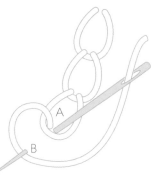

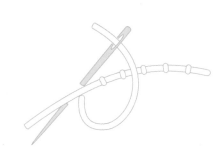

Chain stitch What a wonderful stitch! Once you've learned this, you'll use it over and over. Bring the needle to the front at the desired starting point, A. Holding a small loop of thread with your thumb, insert the needle again, just next to A, bring the point out again a short distance away at B (in the direction your chain is going), looping the thread under the needle before pulling it through. To make the next stitch, insert the needle again next to B, and come out again a short distance away, looping the thread under the needle, as before. To finish, anchor the last loop with a tiny straight stitch.

Couching stitch Couched work is where threads are laid on the surface of a fabric and held in place by tiny stitches made with a different thread. It is a great way to add extra texture and interest to fabric, as you can lay quite thick threads on the background fabric and anchor them in place with a finer thread. Lay the thread along the line of your design and, using another thread in the same shade or a contrast color, stitch the laid thread in place at regular intervals, taking a tiny stitch over the thread.

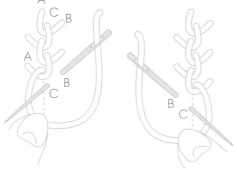

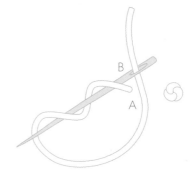

Feather stitch This is a more decorative stitch that follows a desired line and is similar to chain stitch, with the loop remaining open, rather than closed. Bring the needle to the front at the top of the line to be covered (A). Holding the thread down with your left thumb, insert the needle a little to the right at B and take a slanting stitch back to the center, bringing the needle out again at C (which becomes the starting point for the next stitch). To make the next stitch, holding the thread down with your left thumb, insert the needle a little to the left of center, thus reversing the direction of B and C. Continue in this manner, alternating from side to side.

French knot Go dotty with these "knots." Bring the needle to the front at A and, holding the thread taut with one hand, wind the thread around the needle twice (or more, if you want a bigger knot). Keeping the thread taut, insert the needle again close to A, at B. Holding the knot in place with your thumb, pull the thread through to form a firm knot. You can also make thicker knots by using thicker threads.

Screen printing basics

In this chapter, we explain how you can screen print your own fabric for the projects in the following chapters. We really want you to be inspired to try it for yourselves, and then get printing and making for friends and family, as well as yourself. The techniques that we share here are the same ones that we have used daily since 2002, and still use, to create the Prints Charming style.

Screen printing is a way of applying color and design to fabric. As the name suggests, a screen, with a fine silk-like fabric stretched across it, is used to transfer the design. This "silk" allows the ink to be pushed through it by hand with a squeegee. Cut-out paper is transformed into an impervious stencil and, where there is no paper, the ink is pushed through the screen onto the fabric — voilà, a design on the fabric!

At Prints Charming, we develop most of our original designs using a paper-cut method of screen printing. We love this method, as it allows you great freedom and gives immediate, satisfying results.

Paper-cut technique means you can create designs quickly and cheaply, making it ideal for a one-off project as well as for repeat designs. It doesn't have to be tricky, it doesn't have to be hard: it's all about being simple and effective.

The exciting part about the technique we use is the organic, random nature of the results. There will be imperfections, but we see them as part of the handmade process, a part of us, the way we felt on the day, the way the weather was or what music was playing! Remember, out of experimenting arrive the best of surprises.

Getting started

What you will need

❋ **Silk screens in a variety of sizes** These are available from good craft stores — ask for ones that are suitable for printing on fabric. We have no preference for wooden or aluminum frames, and use both. Go for what suits your budget

and size of table, but remember, that as the screens will need to be washed, you should not buy ones that you can't fit in a suitable basin or sink (although you can also wash them out in the yard with a hose, as the inks are fully water-soluble).

✳ **Squeegees to suit the width of your screens** Available where you get your screens.

✳ **Water-based fabric inks** As with the silk screens, you will be able to get these at a good craft store. You can mix the inks to create a range of colors, so a basic selection can turn into many colors and shades.

✳ **Pencils and paper** We use basic photocopier paper for our stencils. After much time and experimentation, we have just found it to be the best for us. You will need a new piece of paper for each motif. The ink gradually causes the paper to deteriorate, but when printing lengths of fabric, you should be able to print about $1^2/_3$–$2^1/_4$ yards of fabric, or about 10 motifs, using the one stencil, before you need to cut another.

✳ **Craft knife** With retractable blade for safety.

✳ **Packing tape** We use clear tape, so you can see through it to the screen.

✳ **Cutting mat** This is to save your table when cutting your screens out with the craft knife.

✳ **Nail brush** This comes in handy to remove excess ink on your screen. The washing of your screens and squeegees is very important, as any ink that stays in the screen will block the mesh and affect the results of your next print.

✳ **Double-sided tape** This is to attach "floating" sections of your cut-out design (that is, sections that are not attached to the rest of the stencil) to the silk screen, to stop them from moving while you print.

Table preparation

You need to prepare the table that you will be printing on. There are two reasons for this. The first is to protect the surface you will be printing on. Secondly, you will achieve a much better printed image if you have prepared the table properly. Stretch two layers of fleece over your table and then a piece of muslin over the top. If you are thinking of setting up a table permanently, you can staple gun the layers to the table. If it's a more temporary set up, stretch your fleece and muslin over your work surface and hold securely in place with several bulldog clips. We suggest you don't use your priceless heirloom dining table for screen printing, covered or not!

Fabrics to print on

We print a lot on white fabric. Colors just sing on a white background and you have more scope for play with color. White cotton fabric, such as a good quality plain homespun, is also cheap and so makes more sense for experimenting on, as well as using as a constant base cloth. Why not practice on an old 100% cotton sheet?

We only print on natural fibers, such as cotton, linen, hemp, or mixes. Different weaves and types of fabrics, such as denims, twills, and "slubby" fabrics, will also give you a different look. Make sure there are no coatings on the fabrics, that is, that they don't feel shiny. If you are unsure, you can wash your fabrics before you print on them, to prepare the surface so the ink remains fast on the fabric.

Heat setting

Heat setting is also a very important part of the fabric printing process and should not be omitted. Heating the ink sets it onto the fabric, making your printed fabric washable. Follow the manufacturer's directions for the ink you intend to use.

Motifs

The motifs we have designed for your use are printed throughout the book. Each of the motifs is for a particular project, but hey, use them for other items in the book, or for ideas of your own! Make use of the photocopier and enlarge or reduce them to any size you like. Use the whole motif or maybe use just a portion of it. Trace them out onto paper, using a window as a light box, but always save the original from the book, so that you have the motif to use over and over again.

We would ask, however, that you use the motifs for your personal projects only. Please do not mass produce them for commercial gain.

Some of the motifs have a line printed around the outside. This gives you the option of having a solid edge on your motif or, if you cut to the line inside the outer line, of having a more defined shape to the motif. This can be an important consideration when printing negative/positive.

Negative/positive printing

When you cut out a motif for printing, the sections that you remove from the paper leave holes where the ink will come through onto the fabric, creating the design, and the remaining solid paper areas prevent the ink from printing. Thus, if you cut away a heart shape from the center of your paper, you will get a heart printed on your fabric in ink. This is known as a positive image. But if you cut out the heart and use this cut-out paper heart on the screen to block the ink, you will get an area of ink surrounding a non-printed heart shape in the center. This is known as a negative image. You can thus create both a positive and negative print of the same design and we often use both, to create variation and interest. A simple way to remember which is which: if the design is printed in ink, then it's positive; if the design shows on the fabric as a non-printed area surrounded by ink, then it's negative.

Step-by-step printing

The following steps describe how we print by hand. You will, of course, develop your own technique, one that suits you and that's great. But once you have started printing, don't stop! This is crucial — if you leave your screens for too long, the ink will set in the screen fabric, ruining your screen. So, no phone calls answered while printing!

STEP 1 Prepare your space, table (see **Table preparation** on page 22 for instructions), fabric and inks for printing.

STEP 2 Trace your chosen motif onto the paper you will use for the stencil, positioning the motif as close to the middle of the paper as possible.

STEP 3 On a cutting mat, cut out the motif accurately, using a craft knife. Remember that where you want the color to come through onto the fabric, there should be a "hole" in the paper.

STEP 4 You now need to attach your motif to the screen. If you have cut parts of a design that are now "floating," that is, they are not attached to any other part of the design, you need to attach small strips of double-sided tape to these floating pieces, so that they will adhere to the screen. To do this, attach the tape while they are lying in their cut position, then simply center the flat side (the right side) of the screen over them and press it onto them as they lie. Rub over the screen gently to ensure good adhesion. You can then flip the screen over with the floating pieces attached and lay the paper from which you cut them on the right of the screen, making sure the motif is in the middle of the screen. (Keeping the motif in the middle means that it is surrounded by a border of paper. This allows for a "well" for your ink when printing, that is, an impervious place for your ink to sit in that is not over your motif.) Now attach the outer edges of the paper to the screen, using the packing tape. Make sure there are no gaps between the paper and the edge of the screen: mask off right to the frame edge, so ink doesn't get on your fabric where you don't want it!

STEP 5 Place the screen, right side down, on your fabric where you want the first image to be printed. Apply some ink to the screen near the top of the screen in the "well."

STEP 6 Using the squeegee, drag the ink over the motif to the other end of the screen at about at 45-degree angle, using a firm, but not heavy, pressure. Now pull the ink back to the end you started at and gently tap the squeegee onto the screen to remove excess ink. Now do what is called an "empty" pull over the motif, that is, a pull of the squeegee with no ink, to remove any excess ink that is lying over the design.

STEP 7 Gently lift the screen to reveal your printed image.

STEP 8 Leave fabric to air dry or use the hair dryer, if needed. (If printing another of the same motif close to the first, or printing other colors over the top, you will need to make sure every layer is just touch dry. A hair dryer will come in handy here.)

STEP 9 Heat set the printed motif, following the ink manufacturer's instructions.

You've now made some printed fabric! Don't forget to wash your screen thoroughly and scrub it with the nailbrush when you have finished, before the ink has a chance to dry out in it. (If you allow the ink to dry in the screen, you will have to buy a new one!)

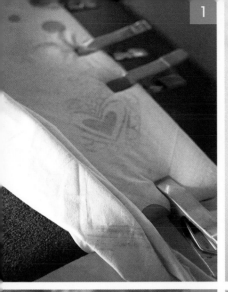

How to print stripes

It's not difficult to print stripes and the technique is the same as the basic method. You just need to remember that you can only print a striped section that fits in your screen (remembering to allow for the "well"), so you are printing crosswise stripes, not lengths. From paper, cut away a series of stripes so that your motif looks like a barred window in the center. You can rule these up, but we like to cut them freehand for a slightly wonky stripe. Attach the paper to the screen with packing tape and print, following the steps on page 24. Simply move the screen across your fabric to create the next sequence of stripes, repeating until you have the amount of printed fabric that you need.

Two colors and overprinting

Once you get used to printing, you can start to experiment with two or more colors, masking off areas of your design and cutting a new stencil for the new color. Just remember that the first lot of ink must be touch-dry before you print the new color. You can also experiment with overlapping sections of designs, creating interesting new colors where the printed sections overlap. A design as simple as different-size circles looks wonderful when the circles overlap. Have fun!

Tip

Once you've gone to the trouble of cutting a stencil, print more fabric than you need and save the extra printed fabric for other projects or for making gifts.

Nursery

Ice blues, grassy greens, canary yellows, with a hint of orange. Calming colors, just right for a baby's nursery.

Heart motif

Baby quilt

This little quilt is constructed in nine rows of nine small squares and is very simple to sew together, allowing you to get on with the fun part of hand-quilting and embroidering.

Measurements

Finished quilt measures approximately 45¹/2 inches square.

What you need

- 8 fat quarters (see **Note**, below), for the quilt top
- ¹/3 yard × 44-inch white cotton fabric (see **Screen printing**, below)
- 3 striped fat quarters, for the binding (we used pale yellow stripe)
- 51-inch square fabric, for backing
- 51-inch square quilt batting
- Rotary cutter, mat, and quilter's ruler
- Sewing thread
- Perle cotton No 8, in white and a variety of colors
- Embroidery needle

Note. We made our quilt using eight of our hand-printed fat quarters, which measure 17³/4 inches square, printed on a 19³/4-inch square of white cotton fabric. We used a white starburst on ice-blue background, white-and-ice-blue stripes, large white spot on pale aqua background, small white spot on pale apple green background, ice-blue starburst on white background, small white spot on canary yellow background, white-and-pale-aqua stripes, and large white spot on pale apple-green background. If you want to screen-print some of your own fat quarters, using the paper-cut technique described on page 24, you will need eight hand-printed fat quarters, as well as the nine Heart motifs.

Screen printing

The Heart motif is reduced for this project. Reduce the motif on your photocopier until it measures about 2³/4 inches across its widest point. Cut nine 6-inch squares from the white cotton fabric. Following the instructions under **Step-by-step printing**, on page 24, print a total of nine Heart motifs, in colors of your choice. We printed four ice-blue, three pale apple-green and two pale aqua hearts.

Not screen printing?

Choose a variety of fabrics in a pretty, coordinating colorway, making sure you choose fabrics with small and large patterns, for interest and contrast. You could also use the motifs from a novelty print fabric as highlight blocks, instead of the Heart motif. Or why not trace the outline of the Heart motif (trace on the solid line) onto contrast fabrics and appliqué them to the background squares?

What you do

Note. 1/4 inch seam allowance is included throughout and all seams are stitched with right sides together.

1. From each of the eight fat quarters, cut nine squares, each 5¹/2 inches. Trim your nine Heart motifs to measure 5¹/2 inches square. You will now have a total of 81 squares.

2. Lay out your nine rows of nine squares, arranging as you go. Don't worry too much about placement — just make sure you don't have too much of one colorway placed too close together in a group.

3. Sew your nine rows together, being careful to keep your rows in the desired order. Iron seam allowances flat in one direction.

4. Now stitch Row 1 to Row 2, Row 2 to Row 3, and so on, till all rows are stitched together. Iron seams in one direction and give it a good press on the right side. Your quilt top is finished.

5. Sandwich the batting between the wrong sides of the backing fabric and the quilt top. Baste the layers carefully together, smoothing out any creases (see **Quilting basics**, on page 14).

6. Using perle cotton No 8 in white, hand-quilt your quilt as desired (see **Quilting basics**, on page 14). We quilted ¹/4 inch along one side of each seam in both horizontal and vertical rows.

7. Now the fun begins. We used perle No 8 threads that reflected the color palette of the fabrics and also a stronger peach as an accent color to highlight the Heart motifs. Using a basic selection of stitches, (see **Stitch guide** on page 16), have fun embellishing and creating unique patterns around the Heart motifs.

8. When all the quilting and embroidery are complete, trim the edges of the batting and backing even with the edges of the quilt top.

9. Now you need to bind the quilt. Cut the striped fat quarters into 4-inch strips (we use a wider than traditional binding), making sure that your stripes go across the 4-inch width, not along the length of the strip. If necessary, trim the strips so there is no plain white showing, and then join them, end to end, into one long strip, keeping the striped pattern correct.

10. Following the instructions under **Quilting basics**, on page 14, bind your quilt.

11. Embroider baby's name and birth date on the back of the quilt.

Tip

You don't need to take your embroidery stitches all the way through to the back of the quilt as your quilting lines are close enough to hold your quilt together. This will make for easier embroidery.

Embroidered heart pillow

This embroidered pillow will look just beautiful in the nursery. Useful on a chair for a new mom, the cuddly shape will also make a lovely soft toy when baby is older.

Measurements

Our finished cushion measures about 13$^1/_4$ x 14$^3/_4$ inches at its widest points, but you can make it any size you like.

You will need

- 20-inch square cotton fabric (see **Screen printing**, below)
- 20-inch square cotton backing fabric
- 20-inch square thin quilt batting
- 20-inch square colored backing fabric (we used a stripe)
- Perle cotton No 8 and/or stranded embroidery floss in a variety of colors
- Embroidery needle
- Sewing thread
- Polyester fiberfill

Screen printing

The Heart motif is enlarged for this project. Enlarge the motif on a photocopier until the heart is about 15$^3/_4$ inches high, or your desired size. Follow the instructions under **Step-by-step printing**, on page 24, to print one Heart motif in the center of your fabric.

What you do

1. If necessary, trim cotton backing and batting to same size as Heart motif panel and baste the three layers firmly together. (Embroidering through the three layers will make your embellishments "stand out" and give the cushion a quilted look.)

2. Use a variety of embroidery stitches and different threads in a range of colors to embellish your Heart motif. We used back stitch, running stitch, and chain stitch to enhance the printed design (see **Stitch guide** on page 16).

3. Once you are happy with your stitching, it is time to add the pillow back. Baste around the heart, along the edge of the printed design. This takes the guesswork out of where to sew when you stitch the front and back of the pillow together.

Not screen printing?

Enlarge the Heart motif to the desired size and trace the outline only onto a piece of fabric. Simply fill in the shape of the heart with concentric lines of embroidery in different colors and stitches. Choose a boldly contrasting fabric in floral or stripe for the back.

4. With right sides together, pin the pillow front and back to each other, and then stitch through all layers, stitching just inside your basting line. Remember to leave an opening on one of the long straight sides. Trim the edges back to 3/8 inch from the stitching line. Snip into the curves and points and turn the pillow right side out. (Snipping across the seam allowance on the curves makes for a smooth line when you turn the pillow right side out. You may have to turn the pillow in and out a couple of times till you are happy with the trimming. You can get quite close to the stitching line without having to worry about it coming undone.)

5. When you are happy with the shape, remove the basting line if it is visible on the outside, and fill the pillow with fiberfill. Turn the raw edges under and slip stitch the opening closed.

Curtains

Delicate voile panels, printed with Heart motifs, are bordered with a wide hem of printed fabric to create curtains with a luminous, ethereal quality. Okay, so the light comes through them and you will probably need a blind as well to darken the room, if necessary, but they're too beautiful not to use.

Measurements

The length and width of the curtains will depend on the size of your windows. Due to the sheerness of the voile, we have chosen to make our curtains in panels the same width as the voile itself, so that there are no seams to spoil the delicate look of the voile section.

You will need

- A quantity of cotton voile
- Purchased print fabric, for border
- Perle cotton No 8, for embroidery
- Embroidery needle
- Sewing thread

Screen printing

The Heart motif is traced at actual size for this project. Follow the instructions under **Step-by-step printing**, on page 24, to print Heart motifs in white ink over the length of voile.

What you do

1. Measure your window to work out the size of your finished curtains. Remember to allow extra at the top for a wide double casing for your curtain rod (the exact amount will depend on the diameter of your curtain rod, but be generous — you can always trim the bottom before adding the border.) If your window is very wide, you may need to consider making more than two drops, depending on the width of your fabric. Voile is inexpensive and you want soft, generous folds, not a stingy, stretched look.

2. Press under 1/4 inch along one raw edge of the voile panels. Now fold over twice the width that you need for your casing and press again. Stitch the pressed edge in place to create a wide hem.

Not screen printing?

This border is a pretty way to add color to plain curtains, regardless of whether you are screen printing or not. If you like, you could also appliqué a motif or two from your border fabric here and there on the voile sections of the curtain, or work lines of running stitch in white or color, to complement the fabric design.

3. Fold the casing in half again from the top, bringing down the top fold to align with the edge that you have just stitched. Press and stitch again through all five layers of fabric. This creates a strong double-thickness casing for your curtain rod.

4. Hang up the curtains so that you can trim them to the right length. The finished border will be 13 inches deep. Allowing for the border (and remembering to add seam allowance), trim your voile to the desired length.

5. Cut your border rectangles, $26^3/4$ inches × the width of your voile, plus $3/4$ inch extra in total, for seam allowance on the width.

6. With right sides together, pin one raw edge of the border fabric to the bottom edge of the voile and stitch, allowing a $3/8$-inch seam. Press seam towards border. Press under $3/8$ inch on the opposite raw edge of the border.

7. Fold the border in half, right sides together, and stitch the sides, allowing $3/8$ inch-seams.

8. Trim the corners and turn the border right side out.

9. Pin the pressed edge of the border in place over the seam and fix in place with a line of decorative running stitch (see **Stitch guide** on page 16). Add extra lines of running stitch to the edges of the voile panel, if desired.

Tip

You could, if you were feeling inspired, screen print your own fabric for the border of the curtains. A line of colored hearts would look very sweet. Why not go all-out and make up a patchwork border to match the baby quilt. Now who's clever?

String of hearts

Embroidered hearts are strung together to make this delicate mobile. Hung in a baby's room, it will fascinate a young imagination as it silently twists and turns.

You will need

- 3 screen-printed Heart motifs (see **Screen printing**, below)
- Colored backing fabric, such as stripes or spots
- Perle cotton No 8 and stranded embroidery floss, in a variety of colors
- Embroidery needle
- Polyester fiberfill
- Sewing thread and needle

Screen printing

One Heart motif is traced at actual size for this project, and the other two are reduced proportionally. Follow the instructions under **Step-by-step printing**, on page 24, to print a total of three Heart motifs, in the colors of your choice, leaving space between each motif. We printed in aqua and green onto a plain white linen/cotton mix.

What you do

1. Use a variety of embroidery stitches and threads in a range of colors to embellish your Heart motifs (see **Stitch guide** on page 16).

2. If you can't see the printing outline on the wrong side of the fabric, baste a stitching line around the heart outline for a guide.

3. Cut a piece of backing fabric to match each embroidered panel.

4. With right sides facing each other, sew each motif and backing fabric together, following tacked line around motif, and remembering to leave a small opening for the stuffing on one straight side.

5. Clip across seam allowance on curves and points and turn hearts right side out. Press each heart, then fill with stuffing. Turn under the raw edges and slip stitch the opening closed.

6. Cut two or three long lengths of perle cotton and thread through the center of the hearts from bottom to top, taking a tiny stitch at the top of each heart to stop it from slipping down the cord. Thread the largest heart first and finish at the top with the smallest. Make a hanging loop in the excess thread extending at the top.

Not screen printing?

Trace the outline of the Heart motif onto a pretty combination of plain fabrics of your choice. Simply fill in the shape of the heart with concentric lines of embroidery in different colors and stitches. You could also use felt for your embroidered hearts, or back your embroidered fabric hearts with felt.

Laundry bag

These bags are handy in whatever size you make them — great for laundry or a spare change of clothes for baby on a day out. Learn to make one and you're sure to be finding all sorts of uses for them.

Measurements

Finished bag measures about 19 inches square.

You will need

- 20 x 43 inches cotton fabric
- Sewing thread
- 1²/₃ yards thin cord
- Safety pin, for threading cord

Not screen printing?

Cut a heart shape from a pretty print fabric and appliqué it to the bag. You could also cut smaller Heart motifs from different fabrics and appliqué a row of hearts across the lower edge of your bag. Appliqué by hand or use fusible web to hold the shapes in place.

Screen printing

The Heart motif is used at actual size for this project. Fold your fabric in half crosswise, so that it measures 19³/₄ x 21¹/₂ inches, and press with the iron to create a crease (bottom edge of bag). Following the instructions under **Step-by-step printing**, on page 24, use the crease as a guide for printing four evenly-spaced Heart motifs along the lower edge on one side of your bag. (Remember to unfold the fabric so that ink doesn't seep through to the other side and spoil your bag). Make sure you have your hearts the correct way up when printing — the bottom of the hearts should point towards the pressed crease.

What you do

1. Zigzag stitch along any raw edges on your screen-printed panel to stop them from fraying.

2. Fold your panel in half crosswise, right sides together, and pin down both sides, starting 3 inches from the top. Allowing ³/₈-inch seams, stitch from this point down both sides, oversewing at both top and bottom to reinforce. Trim corners diagonally at base.

3. Snip across the seam allowance where the seam was started at the top. On each side, double turn the seam allowance under to make a narrow hem that encloses the raw edges. Topstitch in place. Turn bag right side out.

4. Turn under and press ¹/4 inch along each top edge. Fold this pressed edge over again to the inside so that the pressed edge is sitting just above the opening in the side seam. To create a casing for the cord, pin and topstitch two rows of stitching, ¹/4 inch apart.

5. Cut the cord in half and, using the safety pin, thread each length through the topstitched casing. Start each cord on a different side. Knot the ends of each cord together to finish and trim the excess.

Inspiring colors of fuchsia, lilac, lemon, and aqua, combined with wonderful projects, will inspire girls of all ages to get printing and sewing.

Girl's
room

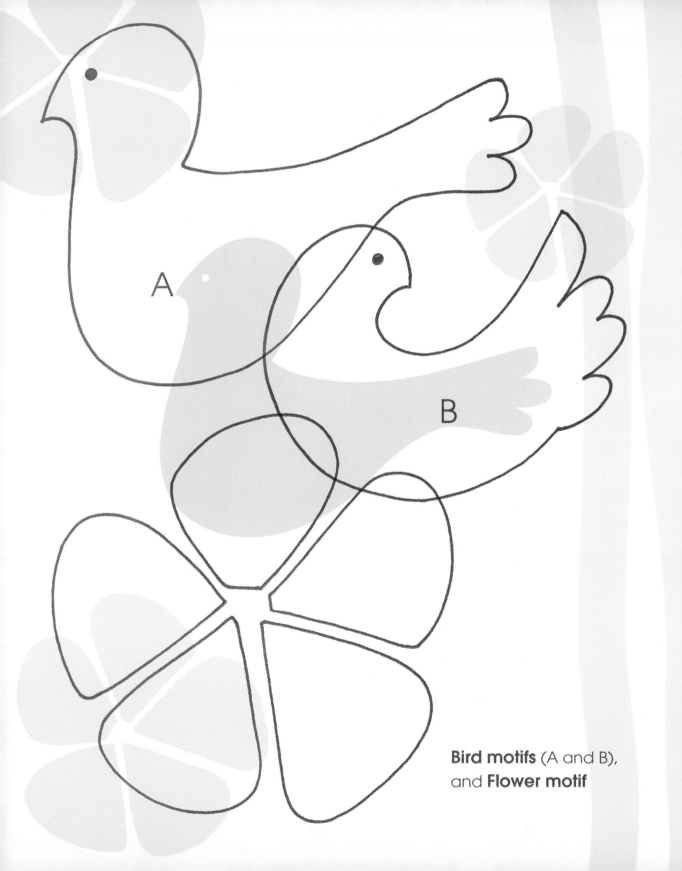

Bird motifs (A and B),
and **Flower motif**

Kimono

The fabric for this kimono was printed as a whole piece, and then simply cut and sewn together. The whole family will want one, not just the girls, so on page 96, we've also made a version to fit adults.

Measurements

To fit a girl aged about 8–12 years.

What you need

- Tracing paper
- Dressmaker's chalk
- 3$1/8$ yards × 44-inch white cotton fabric
- $7/8$ yard × 44-inch contrast fabric, for neckband and tie
- Sewing thread

Pattern pieces

The main pattern pieces for the kimono — front/back and sleeve — are printed on the pattern sheet at the back of the book in one child size (Small) and one adult size (Large). Note that $5/8$-inch seam allowance and 1$1/4$-inch hems, where appropriate, are included on all pieces. Trace the size you need onto tracing paper.

Screen printing

This project uses both Bird motifs (A and B) at actual size, and the Flower motif at actual size as well as slightly smaller. (The size isn't crucial — simply reduce it on your photocopier to make a smaller version of the original.) Before cutting the pattern pieces from your fabric, lay them on the fabric, following Step 1, on page 50, and trace around the pieces with dressmaker's chalk. This is to give you an idea of where the printed motifs will lie on the finished kimono. Following the instructions under **Step-by-step printing**, on page 24, print positive Bird and Flower motifs randomly onto the front/back and also onto the sleeves, if you wish.

Not screen printing?

Make up the kimono in any pretty fabric. You could cut the neckband, tie and maybe even the sleeves from a contrast plain or striped fabric.

Tip

This is a loose-fitting garment that will fit a range of sizes. However, it's very easy to adapt the pattern by increasing or reducing the length of the front/back and the sleeves. When you do this, don't forget to adapt the length of the neckband as well.

What you do

1. Following the layout diagram, below, lay your fabric out in a single layer, pin the pattern pieces to the wrong side and cut out. You should cut one front/back and two sleeves. From contrast fabric, cut one strip, 4 × 94$\frac{1}{2}$ inches for the neckband, and one strip, 4 × 39$\frac{1}{2}$ inches, for the tie. (Both these measurements include $\frac{5}{8}$-inch seam allowance.)

2. Press the neckband in half lengthwise, wrong sides together, then open out again. Now press under $\frac{5}{8}$ inch on one long edge.

3. With right sides together and matching raw edges, pin the unpressed edge of the neckband to the opening edge of the kimono front, from hem edge to hem edge.

4. Stitch the neckband in place as pinned. Fold the band in half along the pressed fold line. Topstitch along the band, near the seam line, securing the pressed edge in place on the inside.

5. With right sides together, stitch the sleeves in place, matching the shoulder marks.

6. Next, sew the side seams in one continuous operation, from cuff to hem edge.

7. Neaten the raw edges of the seam allowance with either zigzag or with overlocking.

8. Double turn the hem and cuffs $\frac{3}{4}$ inch in all — or your desired size — and topstitch in place.

9. Fold tie in half lengthwise, right sides together. Stitch ends and long sides together, leaving an opening in long side for turning. Turn right side out, slip stitch opening closed, and press.

neckband —

tie —

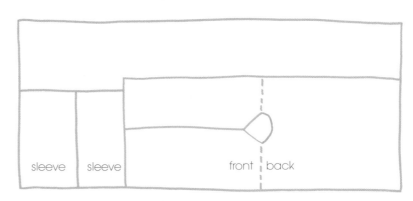

sleeve | sleeve | front | back

Hexagon flower pillow

This Grandmother's Garden flower pillow is the perfect match for a pretty patchwork quilt — but as they're much simpler and quicker to make, why not stitch up a few?

Measurements

Finished pillow measures approximately 22½ inches from straight side to straight side.

What you need

(For each pillow)

- Thin scrap card
- One fat quarter of two different striped fabrics in pink and blue
- One fat quarter in yellow spot
- ⅞ yard × 44-inch backing fabric
- Polyester fiberfill
- Sewing thread
- Covered button
- Long needle

Pattern piece

The pattern piece — hexagon — is printed on the pattern sheet at the back of the book. Trace the hexagon onto thin card and cut out for a template. The traced line will be your sewing line. Remember, when cutting from fabric, to add seam allowance.

Tip

You can make this pillow in a variety of sizes, simply by varying the size of the hexagon template and the size of your screen-printed bird. A pile of different-size pillows on the bed looks fabulous.

Screen printing

Cut out your hexagons, following Step 1, below. The Bird motifs (A and B) are traced at actual size for this project. Following the instructions under **Step-by-step printing**, on page 24, print the motifs onto the pink and blue hexagons, leaving the yellow one plain.

What you do

1. Using your hexagon template, trace a total of seven hexagons onto the wrong side of your fat quarters: three pink, three blue, and one yellow. Cut out, adding 3/8-inch seam allowance around all edges.

2. Using your traced lines as the sewing line, pin and stitch the hexagons together, one after another, into a flower shape, placing the yellow hexagon at the center.

3. Press the finished block well.

4. Using your finished block as a pattern, cut a piece of backing fabric to match the front.

5. With right sides together, sew the back and front together, leaving an opening for turning. Clip the corners and indents, and then turn the cushion cover right side out.

6. Stuff the cushion reasonably firmly with fiberfill and slip stitch the opening closed.

7. Thread your long needle with a triple or quadruple length of sewing thread, for strength. Starting at the center back of the cushion, push the needle out through the center-front hexagon, through the shank of the covered button, and then back down through the cushion again. Pull the thread tightly to dimple the cushion, tie off the threads very firmly at the back, and trim the ends neatly.

Not screen printing?

Make the pillow in a variety of pretty fabrics, choosing small and large prints for contrast and interest. Look for self-cover button kits in craft and fabric stores.

Grandma's star quilt

Inspired by quilts of the 1930s, it's the colors that make this traditional Grandma's Star quilt block anything but traditional! The quilt will take a while to make as each block is probably best pieced by hand, but we think it is well worth the effort. However, if you're new to patchwork, you could make a simpler block, called Grandmother's Garden, which is a flower shape of six hexagons grouped around a central hexagon (see page 51). You could appliqué these hexagon flowers onto plain or striped background squares, and then sew the blocks together to complete your quilt.

Measurements

Finished quilt measures approximately 82 × 58 inches.

What you need

- A mix of pink, yellow, and blue fabrics (we have used a combination of fabrics, but always a yellow in the middle of the block; the exact amount of fabric will depend on how many different fabrics you are using; each block requires five different fabrics)
- Set of Matilda's Own Grandma's Star templates (for stores see page 167)
- 1 7/8 yards × 94-inches backing fabric
- 1 7/8 yards × 94-inches quilt batting
- 3/4 yard × 44-inches binding fabric (we used a blue stripe)
- Sewing thread

What you do

1. Following the instructions that come with the templates, cut and piece 12 complete Grandma's Star blocks, working on the machine or by hand. (As each of the small pieces has to be set in accurately, we find working by hand is easier, although slower. But what's the rush? You're making an heirloom!)

2. Using a completed star block as a template, cut 48 white hexagons for the background. A number of these hexagons will eventually be halved to create the straight edges of the quilt, but we find it easier

Tip

Cut out all your pieces for each block and store them in ziplock bags until it's time to sew them. This means you can take a couple with you in your handbag for a bit of hand stitching wherever and whenever it suits.

to cut whole hexagons, and then trim them back when the quilt top is finished. This allows for slight errors and differences of measurement when the hexagons are pieced — a feature of any good quilt!

3. On a large flat surface (a queen-size bed is good), lay out your hexagons, starting with a vertical left-hand row of 9 white ones (see quilt diagram, below). Now, following the diagram, lay out the rest of the hexagons, noting the position of the patchwork star blocks in each row.

Star block

4. Taking care with the internal angles, sew the hexagons together until you have completed the top.

5. When all the hexagons are joined, press the quilt top well and carefully trim the outer edges into straight lines by removing half-hexagons along the edge. At each corner, you will have a quarter-hexagon. Remember when trimming to leave a seam allowance on the raw edges. Your quilt top is complete!

6. Sandwich the batting between the wrong sides of the backing fabric and the quilt top. Baste the layers carefully together, smoothing out any creases (see **Quilting basics**, on page 14).

7. We had our quilt professionally machine-quilted, using an all-over pattern on the white background and simple in-the-ditch quilting around the central hexagon flowers on the motif blocks. You could, of course, hand-quilt your masterpiece in any way that you like.

8. When all the quilting is complete, trim the edges of the batting and backing even with the edges of the quilt top.

9. Now you need to bind the edges of the quilt. Cut the binding fabric into 4-inch strips, and then join them, end to end, into one long strip, keeping the striped pattern correct if you are using stripes.

10. Following the instructions under **Quilting basics**, on page 14, bind your quilt.

Book covers

Brighten up schoolbooks, sketchbooks, music books, or diaries. No more dreary book covers, and no one will know what you're reading. You won't want to cover this book, of course!

Measurements

The technique can be adapted to any size book.

What you need

- White paper, large enough to cover book (optional)
- A piece of fabric 2 inches larger on all sides than your book
- White glue or tacky craft glue
- Paint brush
- Scissors
- Skewer or satay stick

What you do

1. If your book has a very dark cover, or your fabric is very pale, cover the book neatly first in white paper, before covering it in fabric.

2. Lay out your fabric, wrong side up.

3. Cover the outside of the book sparingly with glue, making sure of good coverage at the edges.

4. Positioning the book spine at the center of the fabric, lower one side of the book onto the fabric.

5. Lift and smooth the fabric to ensure there are no bubbles or wrinkles.

6. Flip the book over so that remaining glued side makes contact with the fabric and repeat the smoothing process.

7. Snip into the fabric on either side of one end of the spine and, using a skewer or satay stick, push this small tab of fabric in under the spine. Repeat at the other end of the spine.

8. Paint glue onto the inside front cover, about 2 inches from the edge. Cut the corners of the fabric at 45-degree angles. Fold over the fabric and stick down on the three sides. Repeat this process on the inside back cover. You can now stick the first page over the fabric edges to neaten.

Trinket-and-treasure hanging

Things to hide and stuff to show off, this hanging allows for both. Only the birds will know your secrets!

Measurements

Our finished hanging measures 38 × 41 1/2 inches. Use our hanging as inspiration for your own and feel free to adapt the measurements, but keep in mind the size of the space where it is to be hung.

What you need

- Thin scrap card
- 1/2 yard × 44-inch striped fabric, for the screen-printed pockets
- 1/2 yard × 44-inch white homespun, for the pocket lining
- 1/4 yard × 44-inch deep purple cotton twill, for the scalloped edge
- 39-inch square yellow denim, for background
- 39-inch square white cotton twill or medium-weight fabric, for the backing
- 1/4 yard × 44-inch fabric, to make a hanging sleeve
- Dressmaker's chalk
- About 2 1/4 yards rickrack trim
- Fabric glue (optional)
- Perle cotton No 8, in colors of your choice
- Embroidery needle
- Sewing thread
- Length of dowel, for hanging

Pattern pieces

The pattern piece for the lower scalloped edge — scallop section — is printed on the pattern sheet at the back of the book. Trace onto thin card and cut out for a template. The traced line will be your sewing line. Remember, when cutting from fabric, to add seam allowance.

Not screen printing?

Trace the Bird motif onto purple cotton twill or even purple felt and appliqué to the pockets, using fusible web or turning under a tiny edge and stitching in place by hand. You could also add a felt or fabric appliquéd scallop edge to the top of each pocket.

The outline for the smaller Scallop motif for screen printing is also printed on the pattern sheet.

Screen printing

The Bird motifs (A and B) are used at actual size for this project. You should also trace the smaller Scallop motif from the pattern sheet. From the striped fabric, cut your pocket rectangles as follows (H × W): two 12 × 7 inches; one 12 × 10 inches; three 8 1/4 × 6 inches; two 6 × 12 inches; one 6 × 8 inches. All measurements include 3/8-inch seam allowance. Following the instructions under **Step-by-step printing**, on page 24, print a Scallop motif onto the top of each pocket rectangle (varying width of scallop to fit width of pieces) and a Bird motif (A or B) onto three or more of the pockets, printing over the stripes.

What you do

1. Cut the plain white pocket lining into pieces to match the printed pockets, that is, (H × W): two 12 × 7 inches; one 12 × 10 inches; three 8 1/4 × 6 inches; two 6 × 12 inches; one 6 × 8 inches.

2. With matching-size pieces and right sides together, sew around the pocket pieces, allowing a 3/8-in seam and leaving an opening in one side for turning. Trim corners, turn right side out, and slip stitch opening closed. Iron flat.

3. Decorate the top edge of each pocket with rickrack (use fabric glue or stitching to hold it in place) and a line or two of running stitch (see **Stitch guide**, on page 16), in the color of your choice.

4. Fold the purple cotton twill in half lengthwise, right sides together. Using dressmaker's chalk, trace a scalloped edge onto the fabric, using your template and flipping it end on end until you have the desired length. Make sure your scallops finish and start at your seam for the main part of the hanging (so you don't get half scallops).

5. Stitch along the chalk line, trim the seam allowance, and clip the curves and indents. Trim and notch carefully here to get a nice smooth scallop, and then turn it right side out.

6. Using perle cotton in a contrast color, work a line of running stitch around the curved edge of each scallop.

7. Press under and stitch a narrow double hem on the shorter raw edges of the hanging sleeve. Press under 5/8-inch on each long raw edge and topstitch the sleeve along both long edges to the top edge of the backing square, about 1 1/2 inches down from the top edge. Instead of stitching the sleeve absolutely flat to the backing fabric, remember to allow a little ease for the diameter of the dowel rod to be inserted.

8. With right sides together and raw edges matching, position the finished scalloped edging on the bottom edge of your background fabric with the scallops facing into the center. Place your backing fabric on top, raw edges matching, and pin. Sew around the edge, allowing a 5/8-inch seam and leaving an opening in one side. Trim corners, turn hanging right side out, slip stitch opening closed, and press well. (We had a nice frayed edge on the selvage of our yellow background fabric, so we made a feature of it, rather than enclosing it in the lower seam.)

9. Now position the pockets on the front of the hanging, thinking about the treasures that will find a home here as a guide to the placement of the pockets. Pin and topstitch in place, close to the finished edges.

10. Insert the dowel through the hanging sleeve, and you're done!

Tip

When trimming a detailed shape like this, you may have to turn it in and out a few times to clip the curves and angles, till you are happy with the shape. It's well worth being slow and steady for a great effect.

Brooches

This is the perfect way to use up fabric scraps. Brooches always look great en masse or, if you can bear to part with them, they make great gifts. Invite friends round for a brooch-making party — with popcorn of course!

Measurements

Finished brooch measures about 4¹/2 inches across.

What you need

- 5 different 5¹/2-inch squares of scrap fabric
- 3-inch square of a contrast print
- 3-inch square of felt, for backing
- Embroidery threads and needle
- Dressmaker's chalk or washable pen
- Decorative button
- Pin back
- Craft glue

What you do

1. Trace the outline for the flower and center (on the pattern sheet) onto scrap card or paper and cut out for templates.

2. Using dressmaker's chalk, trace the flower shape onto the wrong side of your five printed fabric squares and cut out.

3. Trace the center shape onto the right side of the contrast print square, but do not cut out yet.

4. Using embroidery thread and stitches of your choice (see **Stitch guide**, on page 16), embroider inside the traced center, as desired.

5. When all embroidery is done, cut out the center on the traced line.

6. Layer the five flower shapes, one on top of the other, rotating each layer so that the petals can be seen. Top with the embroidered center and stitch all the layers together through the middle.

7. Stitch the button in place through middle and tie off at the back.

8. Trace a center shape onto your felt square, cut out and stitch the pin in the middle.

9. Glue the felt backing circle to the back of the brooch and voilà — you're finished!

Tip

If you have a great button shop nearby, check out their button sizes. With this in mind, embroider or print circles to that size and then have them made into buttons. Some stores will be able to make them into badges as well.

Fly away birdie

Hang this birdie on your door as a decoration or perhaps to indicate to the family that you do not want to be disturbed.

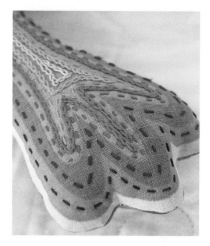

Measurements

Finished bird is approximately 10½ inches long × 8 inches high.

What you need

- 20-inch square plain fabric (see **Screen printing**, below)
- Dressmaker's chalk
- Embroidery threads and needle
- 20-inch square backing fabric
- Sewing machine
- Sewing thread
- Needle
- Polyester fiberfill
- Narrow ribbon, for hanging

Screen printing

The Bird motif (A) is enlarged for this project. Using your photocopier, enlarge the motif until it measures about 10½ inches across the widest point. Following the instructions under **Step-by-step printing**, on page 24, print one Bird motif (A) onto your fabric, leaving at least ¾ inch fabric all round. (Printing on a larger piece of fabric will make for easier embroidery.)

What to do

1. Embellish the Bird motif with embroidery as desired, using a variety of colors and stitches (see **Stitch guide**, on page 16).

2. If the outline of the bird is not clear on the wrong side of the fabric, baste around the outline with sewing thread to give a clear sewing line. If you are using pale fabric, you could also put it on a light box or hold it up against a well-lit window and trace around the outline — on the wrong side of the fabric — in pencil.

3. With right sides together, stitch the embroidered bird and backing together around the outline, leaving an opening for the stuffing. Trim the seam allowance, clip the curves, and turn right side out.

4. Stuff the bird and slip stitch the opening closed.

5. Stitch on a ribbon loop and hang on your door knob.

Not screen printing?

Trace the Bird motif onto plain or printed fabric. Embellish with embroidery — maybe even adding a few pretty beads — and then cut out, adding seam allowance all round. Add the backing and stuff as for the screen-printed bird.

Tip

Overprint two or more successively smaller birds in the center of the first, for a subtle gradation of color.

Boy's room

Starbursts of red, orange, and blue explode onto fabric, making for a boy's room perfect for dreaming and play.

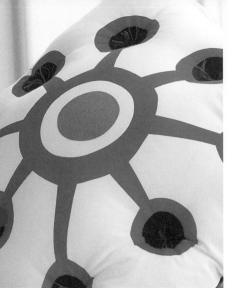
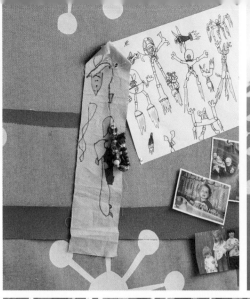

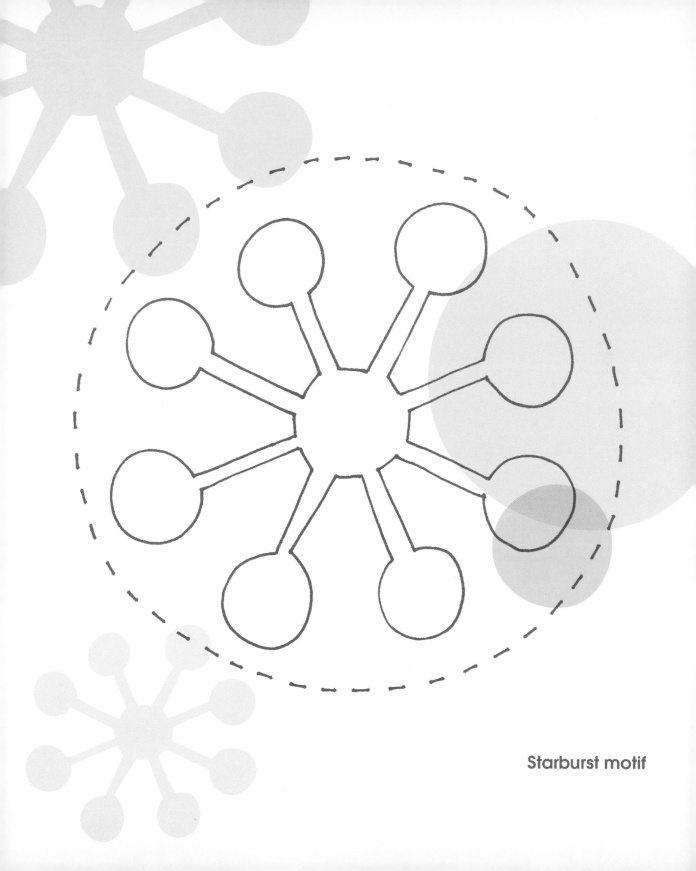

Starburst motif

Pajama shorts and tank

Pajama shorts

Print your fabric and sew the shorts. How wonderful is that! Then add an appliquéd tank top or T-shirt to make a matching pair of very cool PJs. Once you've mastered the technique, every child you know will want a pair.

Measurements

To fit a boy aged 5–6 (7–8, 9–10) years.

What you need

- Tracing paper
- 1¹⁄₈, (1¹⁄₄, 1¹⁄₃ yards) × 44-inch plain lightweight fabric
- Sewing thread
- 1-inch wide elastic, to fit around child's waist

Pattern pieces

The pattern pieces for the shorts — front and back — are printed on the pattern sheet at the back of the book in three sizes. Where appropriate, ⁵⁄₈-inch seam allowance and 1¹⁄₄-inch hems are included on all pieces. Trace the size you need onto tracing paper.

Tip

Add extra length to the pattern pieces to make full-length pants, tapering in to the ankle slightly, if you want to reduce the width at the lower edge.

Screen printing

The Starburst motif is used at actual size for this project and includes the dotted line. Following the instructions under **Step-by-step printing**, on page 24, print negative motifs randomly onto the length of fabric before cutting the pieces.

What you do

1. Fold your fabric in half lengthwise, right sides together, pin the pattern pieces to the wrong side of the double fabric, and cut out. You should cut two fronts and two backs.

2. With right sides together and allowing a $5/8$-inch seam, stitch fronts to backs at side seams.

3. Fold each front/back, right sides together, and stitch the inside leg seam, allowing a $5/8$-inch seam allowance.

4. Neaten the seam allowance with either overlocking or zigzag stitch, to prevent fraying.

5. Turn one of the legs right side out. Put this leg inside the other leg, right sides of fabric facing each other, so that the inside leg seams are matching and the upper raw edges are even.

6. Allowing a $5/8$-inch seam, sew the two sections together from center back to center front. Neaten the seam allowance as before, and turn the shorts right side out.

7. Press under $1/4$ inch around the waist edge. Fold over another $11/4$ inches to form a casing and, starting about $3/4$ inch from the center back, topstitch the casing down all the way around the waistline, stopping $3/4$ inch from the center back. This leaves an opening for you to thread your elastic through.

8. Measure elastic around child's waist, pulling so that it is firm but not too tight. Cut elastic to this measurement, plus $11/4$ inches. Thread elastic through the casing using a safety pin. Overlap the elastic ends by $5/8$ inch and stitch the ends together to secure.

9. Press up $5/8$ inch on the lower edges, press up another $5/8$ inch, and then stitch the hem in place by hand or machine.

Not screen printing?
Sew the shorts in a novelty print cotton fabric and save the scraps to decorate a matching tank with appliqué.

Tank

This technique has so many uses, from individualizing a T-shirt or tank, to creating your own greeting cards, or making art for your walls. Look for the fusible web at your local craft store and then just try to stop yourself!

What you need

- 20-inch square plain fabric (see **Screen printing**, below)
- Double-sided fusible web
- White tank or T-shirt
- Variety of perle cotton No 8 and/or stranded embroidery floss
- Embroidery needle

Screen printing

The Starburst motif is printed at actual size for this project (unless you are printing for a very small tank). Trace the motif (including the dotted line) and, following the instructions under **Step-by-step printing**, on page 24, print one negative Starburst motif in the center of a 20-inch square of fabric. We printed in red ink on an aqua background.

What you do

1. Trim the edges of the fabric back to about 3/4 inch larger than the motif. Cut a piece of fusible web to the same size. Following the manufacturer's instructions, press the web to the wrong side of the fabric with a hot iron until the two are fused.

2. Keeping the motif centered, trace a circle around the motif, about 1/4 inch outside the edge of the motif, tracing on the paper side. Cut out accurately on your traced line.

3. Peel away the backing paper and press the motif into position on the tank or T-shirt.

4. In a color to suit your printing, work a line of running stitch (see **Stitch guide**, on page 16) around the edge of the appliquéd circle. Outline extra features of the design with running stitch, as desired.

Not screen printing?

Cut a circle shape or perhaps a complete motif from your shorts fabric and appliqué to the tank, using fusible web for extra stability and to reduce fraying.

Tip

Although fusible web will hold appliquéd pieces in place without stitching, it is advisable to machine-stitch or hand-stitch them onto a garment so that they will stay in place during repeated washing.

Tufted cushion

Cushions for the bed, or cushions for a chair, cushions for the floor — cushions, cushions everywhere!

Measurements

These cushions can be made in any size, but the pictured example is 24 inches square.

What you need

- Two 24 3/4-inch squares heavier-weight fabric, to withstand the rough and tumble of young boys
- 24-inch cushion form
- Sewing thread and needle
- Safety pins, for basting
- Perle cotton No 8, for "tufting"
- Long needle

Screen printing

The Starburst motif is enlarged for this project. Using your photocopier, enlarge the motif (without the dotted line), until it measures about 19 inches across. Following the instructions under **Step-by-step printing**, on page 24, print one large positive motif in the center of your fabric. For added interest, we masked off a circle in the center of the motif, leaving it white, and then overprinted a smaller, bright blue circle in the center of the white. We then also overprinted the center of each circular "satellite" with a small positive circle in a darker blue. None of this is strictly necessary, but it's not at all difficult and makes the finished cushion more colorful. For the overprinted circles, just cut a circle from the center of a sheet of paper, making it slightly smaller than the diameter of the circle you want to overprint. Center the screen over the circle on your printed fabric and print the smaller circle in a contrast color. Remember to allow the ink to dry before printing the next one.

Not screen printing?

Make large cushions from any sturdy print and tuft at equal intervals — perhaps in a grid pattern — across the surface of the cushion.

What you do

1. With right sides of the fabric together and allowing a $3/8$-inch seam, stitch around four sides leaving an opening in one side.

2. Trim the corners and turn the cover right side out.

3. Insert the cushion into the cover and slip stitch the opening closed.

4. To create the tufts, thread a long needle with perle cotton No 8 thread. From the front of the cushion, take a stitch through the cushion to the back, and then back to the front again, just next to where the thread came out, so you don't "undo" your stitching. Now, pull the threads tightly so that the cushion dimples, and then knot the threads off very securely. Trim, leaving $3/4$-inch ends. Using this technique, make a tuft in each of the little circular "satellites." You could also add one to the center of the cushion.

Tip

The size of the motif on our cushion requires a large screen. If your screen is not large enough, and you don't want to buy another one, don't fret! Simply print a number of smaller motifs onto your fabric.

Sheet set

Quickly liven up a plain sheet set into a more colorful place for heads to rest.

Measurements

We've made a twin sheet set, but you could adapt the measurements as required.

What you need

- Purchased twin bed sheet set
- 3/4 yard × 44-inch colorful print fabric, for border
- Sewing thread

What you do

1. Put the bottom flat sheet or fitted sheet aside.

2. From the top sheet, remove the "leading edge" or hem of the sheet. (If you leave this on it will be too bulky inside your new patterned border.) Measure accurately across the top of the sheet.

3. Cut a piece of your printed fabric that measures the width of your sheet plus 1 1/4 inches × 10 inches.

4. Fold this strip in half lengthwise, right sides facing each other, and press. Allowing 5/8-inch seam allowance, stitch across the short ends, starting (or finishing) each seam 5/8 inch from the long raw edge. Trim corners at fold and turn right side out.

5. With right sides together, pin one raw edge of your printed border to the cut edge of the sheet, then stitch, allowing a 5/8-inch seam. Press the seam away from the sheet.

6. Press under 5/8 inch on the remaining raw edge of the border and turn the border right side out so that the sheet is sandwiched between the layers of the border fabric.

7. Topstitch through all layers to secure the remaining border edge.

Tip

Why not print a pillowcase to match your sheet? We printed overlapping circles and a Starburst motif onto a purchased pillowcase, taking care to avoid the seams. Remember to put something impervious, such as thin card into the pillowcase before printing, to stop the ink bleeding through to the back. Leave it in place until dry.

Starburst quilt

Starbursts of color make for a standout quilt that is sure to be loved. Printing the Starburst motif on different colored fabrics will give your version of this quilt an extra blast.

Measurements

Finished quilt measures 58¹/₄ x 79¹/₄ inches.

What you need

- Nine 21¹/₂-inch squares printed fabric (see **Screen printing**, below)
- 1¹/₄ yards x 44-inch striped cotton fabric in orange/red/grey and white (see **Screen printing**, below)
- ¹/₂ yard x 44-inch plain pale aqua cotton fabric
- 2¹/₃ yards x 60-inch backing fabric
- 2¹/₃ yards x 60-inch cotton batting
- ²/₃ yard x 44-inch coordinating fabric, for binding
- Perle cotton No 8, for quilting
- Rotary cutter, mat, and quilter's ruler
- Sewing thread

Screen printing

The Starburst motif is enlarged for this project — enlarge it on a photocopier until it measures about 14 inches across. Follow the instructions under **Step-by-step printing**, on page 24, to print a total of nine screen-printed Starburst motifs, in the colors of your choice. To add interest to the printed blocks, we printed some of the motifs in negative (see **Negative/positive printing**, on page 23.) We also hand-printed the striped fabric (see **How to print stripes**, on page 27), but you could easily substitute a purchased striped fabric that coordinates with your printed panels.

Note. We used seven Starburst motifs with another two squares of fabric hand-printed with overlapping circles. You can print nine Starbursts or make up the difference with squares in a coordinating fabric — the choice is yours.

Not screen printing?

Choose a variety of interesting, coordinating prints and plains — there are some absolutely gorgeous fabrics available in quilting stores these days — and make up the quilt in the same way.

What you do

Note. 1/4-inch seam allowance is included on all measurements throughout and all seams are stitched with right sides together, unless otherwise indicated.

1. Trim the nine screen-printed starburst panels into 19³/4-inch squares. Arrange them into three rows of three squares and sew the vertical seams on each row. Press seams in one direction.

2. Remove the selvages from your striped fabric (and save them for other things). Cut four 6¹/4 inch-wide strips across the width of the fabric. Join pairs of strips together, end to end, to create two long 6¹/4 inch-wide striped pieces.

3. From striped fabric, also cut two 3¹/2 inch-wide strips and join them together, end to end, into one long 3¹/2 inch-wide strip.

4. From striped fabric, also cut two 1³/4 inch-wide strips and join them together, end to end, into one long 1³/4 inch-wide strip.

6¹/4-inch stripe

starburst blocks

2¹/2-inch aqua
3¹/2-inch stripe

starburst blocks

6¹/4-inch stripe

2¹/2-inch aqua

starburst blocks

1³/4-inch stripe
1³/4-inch aqua

5. Remove the selvages from the plain aqua fabric. Cut two 1³/4 inch-wide strips and four 2¹/2 inch-wide strips across the width of the fabric. Sew pairs of the same width together, end to end, to make three long strips.

6. Following the layout diagram, opposite, stitch one 6¹/4 inch-wide striped strip to the top edge of your first row of starbursts. Trim the edges of the striped strip even with the edges of the panels.

7. Stitch a 2¹/2 inch-wide aqua strip to the bottom edge of the first row of starbursts, and trim edges as before.

8. Stitch the 3¹/2 inch-wide striped strip to the aqua strip and trim.

9. Stitch the next row of starbursts to the striped strip.

10. Stitch the remaining 6¹/4 inch-wide striped strip to the bottom edge of the starburst row, and trim.

11. Stitch the remaining 2¹/2 inch-wide aqua strip to the striped strip, and trim.

12. Stitch the last starburst row in place, followed by the 1³/4 inch-wide striped strip and, lastly, the 1³/4 inch-wide aqua strip.

13. Press all seams in one direction. Your quilt top is complete!

14. Sandwich the batting between the wrong sides of the backing fabric and the quilt top. Baste the layers carefully together, smoothing out any creases (see **Quilting basics**, on page 14).

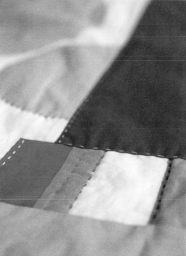

15. Using perle cotton No 8 in a variety of colors, hand-quilt your quilt as desired (see **Quilting basics**, on page 14). We basically emphasised the starburst shape by outline-quilting the circles on our starburst motifs and circle fabric, as well as adding diagonal "starburst" lines between the motif spokes. We added lines of quilting randomly to the striped fabric, following the line of the stripe. On the aqua sashing strips, we quilted close to one seam line. Quilt as the mood takes you and as your fabric pattern suggests!

16. When all the quilting is complete, trim the edges of the batting and backing even with the edges of the quilt top.

17. To bind the quilt, cut seven 3 inch-wide strips across the width of the fabric. With right sides together, join the strips, end to end, to make one long strip. Following the instructions under **Quilting basics**, on page 14, bind your quilt.

Bulletin board

Treasures collected and artworks created should have a special place to be displayed. Here it is.

Measurements

This can be made to fit any size space.

What you need

- Piece of cellulose-based fiber board, the desired size of your bulletin board
- Piece of fabric, large enough to cover board and wrap around to the back (we used the reverse side of denim)
- Scraps of denim in blues that are different to the background
- Double-sided fusible web
- Staple gun and staples

Screen printing

The Starburst motif is enlarged for this project — enlarge it on your photocopier until it measures about 14 inches across. Adhere the denim scraps to your background fabric (see Steps 1 and 2, below) before printing. Following the instructions under **Step-by-step printing**, on page 24, print random positive Starburst motifs in white ink onto the denim background, overlapping the patches wherever you want, in a random fashion.

What you do

1. Lay out your large piece of background denim.

2. Now place the scraps of contrasting denim on the background fabric until you are pleased with the arrangement. Remember, this is a bulletin board, so just a hint of the background will be seen.

3. Apply double-sided web to the wrong side of the denim scraps, remove the backing paper, and fix them permanently in place on the background with a hot iron.

4. You can now screen-print the fabric.

5. When the ink is completely dry, stretch the fabric tightly over the wall board and use a staple gun to affix it to the back.

Not screen printing?

Stretch any colorful purchased fabric over the bulletin board. If you're feeling more creative, you could use plain fabric and appliqué the Starburst motif randomly to the background using the fusible web.

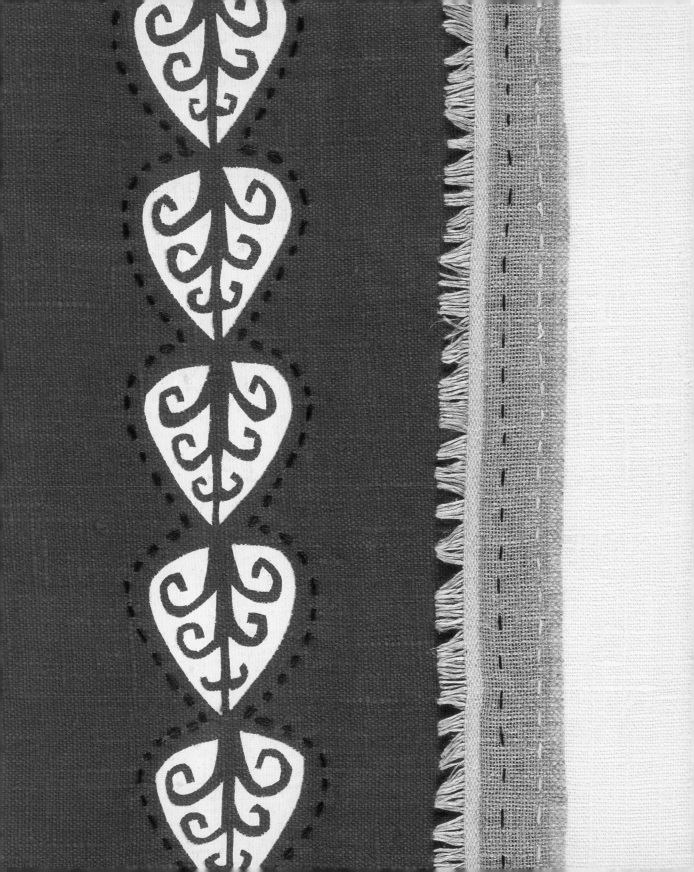

Adult's room

We have designed a Prints Charming Bindi motif that, when used large or small, up or down, will surprise you with the many looks it can be used to create.

Bindi motif

Quilt

Designed around one over-size block, with simple use of the Bindi motif, and then hand-quilted to add extra dimension, the nine blocks in this quilt are quick to stitch together.

Measurements

Finished size 83 × 83 inches. Block measures 28 inches, including seam allowance.

What you need

- 1 yard × 59-inch natural-colored 100% linen (Fabric A)
- $3/8$ yard × 54-inch cream 100% linen (Fabric B)
- $3/4$ yard × 54-inch white linen/cotton shirting weight (Fabric C)
- $12/3$ yards × 59-inch white cotton homespun (Fabric D/E)
- $11/3$ yards × 57-inch natural-colored linen/cotton (Fabric F)
- $1/2$ yard × 59-inch denim blue 100% linen (Fabric G)
- 94-inch square backing fabric
- 94-inch square quilt batting
- $7/8$ yard × 44-inch binding fabric (we used a stripe)
- Matching sewing thread
- Perle cotton No 8, in colors to match fabrics and inks, for quilting

Screen printing

The Bindi motif is traced at actual size, and also enlarged, for this project. On a photocopier, enlarge the motif until it is approximately 11 inches high. Cut the fabrics, following the instructions under **Cutting**, on page 94. Following the instructions under **Step-by-step printing**, on page 24, print the motifs as follows: on one end of each of the nine Fabric C rectangles, print an actual-size denim blue motif; on the nine Fabric F rectangles, print six enlarged red motifs and three enlarged white motifs in the center of the fabric.

Not screen printing?

This is a simple and quick block to construct and looks very effective in a mixture of plain and feature fabrics. Use purchased fabrics and fat quarters to make your own version.

Tip

Screen print purchased 100% cotton pillowcases to match your quilt. Following the instructions under **Step-by-step printing**, on page 24, print the Bindi motif onto the pillowcases, taking care to avoid the seams. Remember to put something impervious, such as thin card, into the pillowcase before printing, to stop the ink bleeding through to the back. Leave the card in place until dry.

Cutting

From Fabric A, cut 9 rectangles, each 28 × 5¼ inches.
From Fabric B, cut 9 rectangles, each 8¼ × 6¼ inches.
From Fabric C, cut 9 rectangles, each 12½ × 8¼ inches.
From Fabric D/E, cut 9 D-rectangles, each 8¼ × 10¼ inches.
From Fabric D/E, cut 9 E-rectangles, each 10½ × 13¾ inches.
From Fabric F, cut 9 rectangles, each 15½ × 14¾ inches.
From Fabric G, cut 9 rectangles, each 5¼ × 13¾ inches.

What you do

Note. 1/4-inch seam allowance is included throughout and all seams are stitched with right sides together unless otherwise indicated.

1. Following the block diagram, opposite, stitch a B and D piece to either side of a C rectangle, along the 8$\frac{1}{4}$-inch edge. Press all seams in one direction.

2. Stitch rectangle A to the top edge of the B/C/D section.

3. Stitch piece E to piece G along the 13$\frac{3}{4}$-inch edge. Press the seam allowance towards the darker fabric.

4. Stitch this E/G section to the longer edge of the printed F rectangle. Press seam allowance towards piece F.

5. Finally, stitch the E/G/F section to the bottom edge of the A/B/C/D section to complete the block. Press well.

6. Construct the remaining eight blocks in the same way.

7. Lay out the nine blocks in three rows of three. Turn the blocks so that the motifs are pointing in different directions and different sections of each block are adjacent to one another. When you are happy with the arrangement, stitch the blocks together into rows of three, and then join the three rows to complete the quilt top. Press well.

8. Sandwich the batting between the wrong sides of the backing fabric and the quilt top. Baste the layers carefully together, smoothing out any creases (see **Quilting basics**, on page 14).

9. Using perle cotton No 8, hand-quilt your quilt as desired (see **Quilting basics**, on page 14). Using red, blue, and natural linen colored threads, we quilted close to the seam lines of the patchwork and across the blocks in places, and then outline-quilted the Bindi motifs.

10. When all the quilting is complete, trim the edges of the batting and backing even with the edges of the quilt top.

11. Cut the binding fabric into 4-inch strips and join them, end to end, into one long strip, keeping the striped pattern correct, if you are using striped fabric.

12. Following the instructions under **Quilting basics**, on page 14, bind your quilt.

Kimono

This kimono is constructed exactly the same as the Girl's Kimono, on page 48. The Bindi motif is printed around the hem line before the garment is constructed.

Measurements

This is a loose-fitting garment, to fit bust 32–36 inches.

What you need

- Tracing paper
- 3⅞ yards × 44-inch natural-colored linen/cotton fabric
- Sewing thread
- Embroidery thread and needle

Pattern pieces

The main pattern pieces for the kimono — front/back and sleeve — are printed on the pattern sheet at the back of the book in one child size (Small) and one adult size (Large). Where appropriate, ⅝-inch seam allowance and 1¼-inch hems are included on all pieces. Trace the size you need onto tracing paper.

Tip

This loose-fitting garment will fit a range of sizes, but to make it longer or shorter, simply lengthen or shorten the pattern pieces. When you do this, don't forget to adapt the length of the neckband as well.

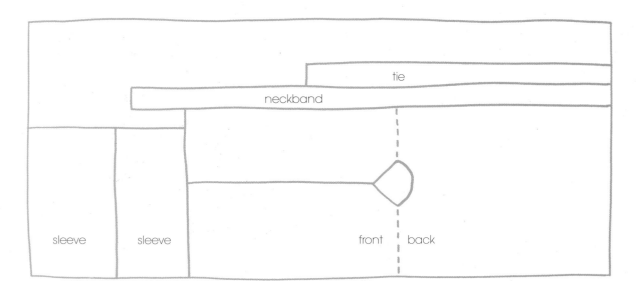

Not screen printing?

Make up the kimono in any plain or printed fabric. For added interest, you could cut the neckband and tie from a contrasting plain, printed, or striped fabric.

Screen printing

This project uses the Bindi motif at actual size. Cut the pattern pieces from your fabric, following Step 1, below. Following the instructions under **Step-by-step printing**, on page 24, print positive Bindi motifs around the hem edge of the front/back. We printed our motifs in white on the natural background.

What you do

1. Following the layout diagram, below, lay your fabric out in a single layer, pin the pattern pieces to the wrong side and cut out. You should cut one front/back and two sleeves. You should also cut one strip, $5^1/_2 \times 113$ inches for the neckband, and one strip, $5^1/_2 \times 61^1/_2$ inches, for the tie. (Both these measurements include $5/_8$-inch seam allowance.)

2. See Girl's Kimono, on page 48, for sewing instructions.

3. When the garment is complete, work around the lower row of Bindi motifs in running stitch (see **Stitch guide** on page 16) for a pretty finishing touch.

tie

neckband

sleeve   sleeve   front   back

N

Scarf

Not only for keeping your neck warm, these scarves make great belts or head scarves as well. Simple to make, they are easy to whip up for presents. We love a frayed edge, so these are made to be washed and scrunched.

Measurements

Our scarf measures about 9½ x 71 inches, but you can adapt the measurements to suit your needs or your fabric.

What you need

- ⅝ yard x 51-inch voile or lightweight cotton, for scarf
- 24-inch square medium-weight linen or linen/cotton mix, for border
- Sewing thread
- Embellishments (these could be embroidery threads, braids, strips of fabric — use whatever takes your fancy)

Screen printing

The Bindi motif is traced at actual size for this project. Press your lightweight fabric in half lengthwise and open out again. This will mark the finished width of the scarf. Following the instructions under **Step-by-step printing**, on page 24, print a series of positive motifs down one side of the fabric, positioning them midway between the fold and the raw edge. We printed navy blue Bindi motifs onto red fabric. We also cut our natural-colored linen in half and printed it with navy stripes (see **How to print stripes**, on page 27), but you could also leave it plain or use a purchased stripe. And for something completely different, why not leave the scarf length plain and hand-print your border fabric?

Not screen printing?

Add interesting bits of purchased fabric to the ends of your scarf. Anything goes here, so just do what looks nice, and embellish it in any way that inspires you: patchwork, embroidery, beading, appliqué — get the idea? Go for it!

What you do

1. From your linen fabric, cut two rectangles, 19³/₄ x 7 inches.

2. With right sides together and allowing ³/₈-inch seams, sew a linen rectangle to each end of the printed cotton. Press seams towards the linen.

3. Fold the piece in half lengthwise and sew the long edges together, using a ³/₈-inch seam allowance.

4. Turn the tube right side out and press flat. This completes the basic scarf — we like to leave the ends open and allow them to fray gently, but if this doesn't suit your look, you could always stitch across both ends as well as the long edge, leaving a small opening for turning.

5. Now the fun part: embellishing and creating your own look. We stitched the cut-off selvages from a piece of fabric to this particular scarf because they look frayed and gorgeous, but you can use anything: hand-printed or purchased fabric strips, circles of fabric, or even appliquéd bindis. You can also add embroidery to your scarf if you feel like it (see **Stitch guide** on page 16). Don't worry about hiding the starting or finishing knots — show them off to create even more interesting texture.

Big cushions and lampshade

Cushions

How wonderful does this look? The same motif printed large in white and smaller in navy. Show off your hand-printed fabric by sewing together some big, comfy cushions. We printed a 27^1/$_2$-inch length of 55-inch fabric to make two 26^1/$_2$-inch square cushions.

Measurements

Finished cushions measure 26^1/$_2$ inches square.

What you need

(For 2 cushions)
- ^{3}/$_4$ yard × 55-inch natural-colored linen or linen/cotton blend
- ^{3}/$_4$ yard × 55-inch fabric, for backing
- Two 18-inch dress zippers
- Sewing thread
- Zipper foot
- Cushion forms to fit
- Embroidery thread and needle, optional

Screen printing

The Bindi motif is traced both at actual size (negative) and enlarged (positive) for this project. Enlarge the positive motif on your photocopier until it is approximately 11 inches high. Following the instructions under **Step-by-step printing**, on page 24, print the larger positive motifs in white on the linen fabric, using the photograph as a guide to placement. Print the smaller, negative motif in navy in the spaces between the white motifs.

Not screen printing?
Make these cushions from any pretty fabric to match your décor. Why not stitch the front together from a number of coordinating fabric scraps, to make a big patchwork cover?

Tip

Use plain fabric for the backs of your cushions in order to make your hand-printed fabric go twice as far.

What you do

1. Before sewing the front to the back, you might like to embellish the Bindi motifs with a little simple running stitch (see **Stitch guide** on page 16). It looks lovely, but is entirely optional.

2. Cut both cushion fabric and backing in half crosswise and trim into matching squares if necessary. Neaten the edges of both by overlocking or zigzagging around all edges. Arrange into back/front pairs and set one pair aside.

3. Place remaining pair together, right sides facing each other and raw edges matching. On wrong side of fabric, mark length of opening for zipper (approximately $1/2$ inch above and below the metal stops on zipper).

4. Put the zipper aside and, allowing a $5/8$-inch seam, sew the seam closed at each end, from your mark to the edge, leaving the seam open in the middle. Press the seam allowance open, pressing open the edges of the unstitched section as well.

5. With the right side of the fabric facing upwards, position your closed zipper under the opening (make sure it's facing up the right way) and pin it in place. Pin one folded edge of the opening about $1/16$ inch from the zipper teeth and pin the other side about $3/8$ inch from the folded edge. Place a pin across the seam at the top and bottom of the opening, setting one pin just above the pull tab and the other just below the zip stop. It is a good idea to baste the zipper in position now before stitching it, as the pins can get a bit awkward while you stitch.

6. Using a zipper foot on your machine, sew the zipper in place, stitching along both sides and pivoting on the needle at the corners to stitch across the top and bottom too. This is called a lapped zipper.

7. Open the zipper and, with right sides together, stitch the cushion front and back to each other around the remaining edges, allowing $5/8$-inch seams.

8. Trim corners, turn right side out through zipper opening and press.

9. Insert cushion form into cover.

10. Repeat process for second cushion.

Lampshade

There are plenty of ready-made lampshades that you can customize into a very elegant, unique piece.

Measurements

Use a cylindrical lampshade of your choice in any size.

What you need

- One plain linen-covered lampshade
- Small amount good quality, open-weave linen to match your shade
- Thin card, for making a stencil
- Fabric paint or screen printing ink (we used white)
- Stencil brush
- Spray adhesive and fabric glue

What you do

1. Look at your lampshade to work out where you would like to add a printed circle and make a tiny, faint mark in each spot.

2. Trace small circles of three different sizes onto the center of three squares of thin card and carefully cut away the traced circle on each piece to create simple stencils.

3. Spray one side of your stencil lightly with spray adhesive and position it on the lamp, over one of your marks.

4. Using fabric paint and a stencil brush, carefully dab paint onto the lampshade through the stencil. Use a dabbing motion rather than brush strokes and don't load the brush with too much paint. It is better to add a second layer of color after the first than to create drips with excess paint. Carefully lift the stencil cleanly away and allow the paint to dry before adding the next circle to the shade.

5. Stencil a few circles of different sizes onto the linen fabric, leaving enough space in between each one for fraying, and allow to dry.

6. Trace a larger circle around your linen circles (this will be the width of your frayed border) and cut out along the traced line. Gently fray the fabric back to the printed circle.

7. Taking care to avoid the frayed edge, glue the frayed circles to the lampshade where desired, to create a fabulous 3D look.

Tip

If stenciling is not your cup of tea, why not simply cut circles from one or two contrasting shades of linen, fray the edges, and glue to your lampshade? You could also cut the plain circles from a closely woven fabric (that is less likely to fray) and glue them in place too.

Headboard

Maybe you don't have a headboard, or your old one needs an update. Create the new focal point of the bedroom with your own fabrics. What's great about this slip-on headboard cover is that it can easily be removed if it needs washing, or you can make two covers and switch them about to change the look of your room occasionally.

Measurements

Technique can be adapted to any size bed.

What you need

- One 94$^{1}/_{2}$ × 47$^{1}/_{4}$ × $^{3}/_{8}$-inch MDF or plywood sheet (cut to your required size, see Step 1, below)
- Medium-grade sandpaper
- 60-inch square thick batting (if you like extra padding, you will need to double this measurement)
- Staple gun
- 1$^{3}/_{4}$ yards × 60-inch medium- to heavy-weight fabric (see **Note**, below)
- 1$^{3}/_{4}$ yards × 60-inch medium-weight fabric, for backing
- Sewing thread
- Universal brackets (to attach headboard to bed)

Note. We used a purchased hand-printed stripe. It's not really feasible to screen print striped fabric of this width at home, but there are wonderful hand-printed furnishing fabrics available to buy. If you want to print your own, why not print the Bindi motif to match the quilt? Since the back of the headboard is not going to be seen, you might want to make it from a plain, less expensive fabric.

Tip

Make your headboard from any bold geometric print. Since it's not an enormous amount of fabric, look for something really special.

What you do

1. Measure the width of the bed with the sheets and quilt on.
(You need to measure the bed while it is made up, because the
headboard should be in proportion to this, rather than to the mattress
alone.) The height should be about 35 inches taller than the top of
the mattress, but the height and shape can easily be adjusted to suit
the proportion of your bed and the room itself.

2. Cut your MDF to the required size — ours was $54^1/2$ inches wide ×
$47^1/4$ inches high. (Many hardware stores will cut the MDF for you for
a few extra dollars.)

3. Sand off any rough edges.

4. Position the MDF in the center of the batting. Mark about 4 inches
extra all round the edges of the MDF, then cut out the batting.

5. Replace the MDF in the center of the batting. Pull the edges of the
batting to the back of the MDF and staple-gun them in place. If you
are using a second layer of batting for extra cushioning, attach it in
the same way.

6. Lay the batting-covered MDF face down on your fabric and mark
an extra 4 inches around all edges. Cut the fabric to this size, then cut
a piece of backing fabric to the same size.

7. Pin the two fabric pieces together, right sides facing each other,
leaving the bottom edge open. While it is still inside out, pull the
pinned cover over the padded headboard, to test the fit, as it's
important that it should fit snugly. Adjust the pins if necessary, and
stitch the seam around the top and sides, leaving the bottom edge
open. Trim any excess seam allowance, trim off the corners, and turn
the cover right side out. Try it on the padded board again to make
sure it fits.

8. Finish the lower edge with a double hem.

9. Attach the headboard to the bed with universal brackets. Screw
one side of the bracket onto the headboard and then attach the
other side to the underside of the bed, or remove the bed's castors,
slip the bracket in place, and re-screw the castors.

Tip

For a tailored look, you could add piping to the edge of your headboard. Sew it to the right side of the printed fabric, using a zipper foot, before stitching the front and back together.

Living room

Print your own paisley and then mix it with printed plains. Hand stitch to highlight motifs and your living room is transformed.

Paisley motif

Patchwork throw and pillow

Patchwork throw

This throw is a play on color. Instead of printing motifs, we overprinted plain-colored linen: you'll be amazed how the same color can change when printed on different base fabrics, giving wonderfully subtle gradations of tone. Gather a selection of linen fabrics in complementary colors, and go for different weights and textures as well, to create a more interesting surface. We made this throw without a sewing machine, so once you have cut all the pieces out, you can sew anywhere. How nice to look at the finished throw and remember where and when you sewed the top together.

Measurements

Finished throw measures about $37\frac{3}{4} \times 39\frac{1}{2}$ inches.

What you need

- A mix of different-weight linen fabrics in a variety of complementary colors (see **Screen printing**, below)
- 44-inch square linen, for backing
- 44-inch square cotton batting
- $\frac{1}{3}$ yard x 44-inch matching linen, for binding
- Sewing thread
- Perle cotton No 8, for quilting

Screen printing

We didn't use a printed motif for this project. Instead, cut a rectangle from the center of your motif paper (leaving the "well" at each end.) If you are using a small screen, your rectangle should be the same size as, or a little larger than the cut pieces, that is, $3\frac{3}{4} \times 5\frac{3}{4}$ inches. If you are using a bigger screen, you can print a larger piece of fabric, then cut it into several rectangles — making the printing job much quicker. Choose a pleasing combination of three or so ink colors (we used terracotta, raspberry and teal) and screen print your linen pieces in these colors, following the instructions under **Step-by-step printing**, on page 24. Print the same color onto a variety of background fabrics, so that you can see how the tone changes subtly, depending upon the color and weave of the fabric.

Not screen printing?

Make the same throw from a range of closely toned purchased plain fabrics. If you are interested in fabric dyeing, it would also be interesting to dye your own pieces of linen, varying the strength of the dye to achieve the subtle color changes that make the throw so effective.

What you do

1. Cut your printed linen into 3³/₄ × 5³/₄-inch rectangles. We cut some rectangles from unprinted, natural-colored linen, for contrast. You need 88 rectangles in all.

2. Arrange the rectangles randomly, on a table or floor, into 11 rows of eight rectangles.

3. Once you are happy with the layout, stitch your pieces together, allowing ¹/₄-inch seam allowance. (Remember, we pieced our rectangles by hand, but if time is pressing, you could always resort to the machine.) Press all seams in one direction on the first row, and then in the opposite direction on alternate rows.

4. Now join your rows together. (If you have to pack up, before you've finished sewing everything together, take a photograph with your digital camera or cell phone so that you can refer to it later.) Press all seams in one direction. Your quilt top is complete!

5. Sandwich the batting between the wrong sides of the backing fabric and the quilt top. Baste the layers carefully together, smoothing out any creases (see **Quilting basics**, on page 14).

6. Using perle cotton No 8, hand-quilt your quilt as desired (see **Quilting basics**, on page 14). We quilted using a linen-colored perle No 8 thread, quilting ¹/₁₆ inch from the seams.

7. When all the quilting is complete, trim the edges of the batting and backing even with the edges of the quilt top.

8. Now you need to bind the edges of the quilt. Cut the binding fabric into 3-inch strips and then join them, end to end, into one long strip.

9. Following the instructions under **Quilting basics**, on page 14, bind your quilt.

Tip

If you stand above the layout and squint your eyes, you will "see" if any of the rectangles stand out and need to be changed.

Patchwork pillow

Make a couple of pillows to match your throw — they do wonders for a tired sofa. Decide on the size you would like to make — as these are not square pillows, you can simply make the size that suits and fill with stuffing.

Measurements

Our pillow measures about 17 x 19 inches, but you can adapt the size to suit your needs.

What you need

- A variety of linen fabrics, printed as for the **Patchwork throw**, on page 114
- Linen backing fabric
- Sewing thread
- Sewing machine (optional)
- Perle cotton No 8, for quilting
- Polyester fiberfill

What you do

1. Cut the number of printed and plain rectangles required for your pillow — we used 20 in all.

2. Arrange the rectangles into order — we used four rows of five rectangles.

3. Allowing ¼-inch seams, stitch your rectangles together as arranged and press well.

4. Using perle cotton No 8 in a natural linen color, sew lines of small running stitch (see **Stitch guide** on page 16) along the seam lines to reflect the quilting in your throw.

5. Cut a piece of backing fabric to match the pillow front and, with right sides together, sew the back to the front around all edges, leaving an opening in one side for turning.

6. Trim corners, turn right side out, and press.

7. Fill cover with fiberfill and slip stitch opening closed.

Tip

If you think that your pillow cover is going to need frequent washing, stitch your own cushion insert from muslin and stuff it with fiberfill. Add a lapped zip to your cover (see **Big cushions**, on page 102) and you will then be able to remove and replace the patchwork cover quickly and easily when necessary.

Footstool

Using the original fabric from an item of furniture is the easiest way to make a pattern if you want to re-cover it. However, re-covering furniture can be tricky, so if you're a novice, choose something simple, rather than your heirloom Chesterfield!

What you need

- Footstool, to be re-covered
- Tracing paper
- Fabric, for re-covering
- Perle cotton No 8, for embellishment
- Embroidery needle
- Sewing thread

Screen printing

Following Steps 1 to 5 on page 120, prepare your fabric piece/s. Depending on the size of your project, you may want to cut the piece/s after you have printed your fabric, or print the fabric after they are cut to size. Adapt the size of the motif to suit your project and, following the instructions under **Step-by-step printing**, on page 24, print motifs onto fabric in one or more colors. We printed the Paisley motif at actual size in navy on the reverse side of a piece of denim.

Not screen printing?
Choose any upholstery fabric that complements your decor, then customize it by adding embroidery around elements of the design. It looks gorgeous.

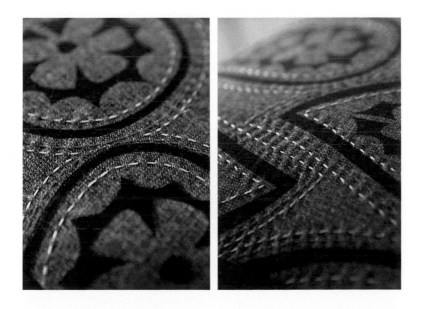

What you do

1. Carefully remove the original cover, making sure you don't rip or stretch the fabric. Stretching will distort the pattern, making a pattern piece that will be too big for your chair or stool. Make a note of any extras you might need for your new cover, such as a zipper or upholstery tacks or braid.

2. Gently unpick any seams if necessary, press lightly with your iron, and lay the fabric pieces onto tracing paper. Trace around the pieces to create your new pattern pieces.

3. If your cover consists of more than one piece, mark on the paper patterns which piece is which, such as chair back, chair seat, and so on. You should also draw an arrow on your pattern pieces to indicate the direction of the straight grain on the original fabric. Make a note of how much seam allowance is included: remember that the original seam allowance may have been trimmed somewhat after sewing, so if this seems to be the case, add extra seam allowance to your traced line, noting how much you have added beyond the stitching line.

4. You will now be able to work out how much fabric you will need for your new covers.

5. Lay your pattern pieces on the wrong side of the new fabric and cut out.

6. We highlighted the motif on our fabric with a line of running stitch (see **Stitch guide**, on page 16) around the outline, using perle cotton No 8. Obviously, if you are going to embellish your fabric in any way, you need to complete it before proceeding with the final construction of the cover.

7. With right sides facing each other, pin the pieces of your new cover together and try it on the stool or chair for size while it is still inside out.

8. Adjust if necessary, and then sew the pieces as pinned.

9. Fit the new cover onto your chair or stool and think about how clever you've been!

Wall art

Stretch your printed fabric over artist's stretchers to create artwork to suit the colors and size of the room where they are to hang. Our examples are intended as inspiration only, so don't feel the need to copy them slavishly. Explore your own creative side and go where the journey takes you!

Measurements

This can be any size that suits your room.

What you need

- Artist's wooden stretcher or stretched canvas frame (from an art supplies store)
- Piece of firm background fabric (bigger than your stretcher so you can wrap this around when finished)
- Staple gun
- Staples

Screen printing

On our piece of fabric, we screen printed a series of different-sized organic rectangles in three colors, overlapping them to create even more colors. But this is just one idea — you could also play with the Paisley motif in different sizes and colors.

What you do

1. When you have finished printing your fabric, stretch your artwork evenly over the stretcher or canvas frame and staple the excess fabric in place at the back.

2. Hang your work and admire.

Not screen printing?

You can create a similar effect to printing by building up a series of appliquéd fabric shapes on your fabric background. Work out your design on a large sheet of paper, cut out your shapes from different fabrics, and machine-stitch them to the background fabric, about 2 inches from the edge of the fabric. You don't need to turn the edges under — let them show. Build up the layers, by adding more shapes in other colors, then stretch the finished piece over the stretcher and hang.

Tip

Since your embroidered fabric is to be stretched over a frame when it is finished, you might find it easier to stretch the fabric in an embroidery hoop while you're working on it so that you can get an idea of what the final effect will be.

Be inspired!

Choose fabrics that you feel complement each other, mixing textures, as well as prints and plains. When you're sewing fabrics together, work some of the seams in the "traditional" way, so that no edges are visible, but stitch others so that the fabrics overlap, showing a raw edge or two. (Use a smaller machine stitch so that when the artwork is stretched over the canvas, your work doesn't pull apart at the seams.) Fray the edges where you think it would look nice, or print one or more motifs onto your fabric — in the center of a plain piece of fabric, or over your patchwork joins. There are no rules. Embroider to your heart's content, using threads, colors, and stitches as the mood takes you. When you think you've done enough, do a bit more! Give yourself the freedom to experiment and possibly make mistakes. We bet that once you've made one of these wonderful pieces, you'll be starting another in no time.

Kitchen

Turn everyday objects, such as aprons, tea towels, and table linen, into little works of art that will make you smile whenever you use them.

Candelabra motif

Tea towels

For this project, collect tea towels from anywhere. Update the ones in your cupboard, buy second-hand ones at markets (the old ones are usually better linen), or new ones. Simply overprint the fabric with a new design. Save time by printing a few at once and then putting them away for a later date. You can also start from scratch and make your own tea towel.

Measurements

If you're making your own tea towel, take the opportunity to make generous ones. Ours are about 39 × 20 inches.

What you need

- 1 1/8 yards × 44-inch linen (this is enough for two tea towels)
- Sewing thread

Screen printing

The Candelabra motif (without the dotted line), or sections of it, can be used at any size for this project — print it actual size or reduce it to print several motifs in a combination of sizes. Remove the selvages from the linen and cut it in half lengthwise, giving two pieces, about 39 × 21 1/4 inches. Print the fabric before you hem it, so that you're not printing over "ridges" made by hemming. Following the instructions under **Step-by-step printing**, on page 24, print positive Candelabra motifs in one or several colors and sizes onto your linen, as desired.

What you do

1. Allowing 5/8 inch in total, double hem the long sides.

2. Now double-hem each end in the same way, or fray the ends, if preferred (see **Tip**, at left).

Not screen printing?

Appliqué bold, colorful shapes to your tea towel fabric. This is especially effective on tea towels that have been stained or damaged in some way.

Tip

You can fray the ends instead of hemming, if you like — we love fraying! Hem the sides, starting and finishing 3 inches from each end. Now stitch across both ends at this 3-inch mark. Use a pin to fray the edges to the 3-inch mark.

Apron

Practical and stylish in the kitchen, aprons are still very popular, so make them for yourself or for the kids. As with the tea towels, make a few and you will have wonderful handmade gifts on hand for whenever the need arises.

Measurements

Small size fits a 4–6 year-old child; large size (measurements in parentheses) fits an adult. Finished apron measures 20 (29) inches long × 16^1/2 (24) inches wide.

What you need

- Tracing paper
- ^{1}/2 (1^1/8) yard × 44-inch lightweight canvas, twill, or linen
- One fat quarter, for pocket (optional)
- 2^1/4 (2^3/4) yards × ^{5}/8-inch woven twill tape
- Sewing thread

Pattern pieces

The pattern pieces for the apron — apron and pocket — are printed on the pattern sheet at the back of the book, in two sizes (child and adult). Note that ^{3}/8-inch seam allowance is included on the curved edge of the apron and on the pocket, and ^{3}/4 inch is allowed on the straight edges of the apron. Trace the size that you need onto tracing paper.

Tip

Screen print the fabric for the pocket. We've used multiple small Bindis (see page 91).

What you do

1. Pin the pattern onto your fabric and cut out the apron shape. Fold fat quarter in half and cut two pockets.
2. Double hem the sides using ^{3}/4-inch allowance (in total) and topstitch. Now double hem the curved edges up to the neck edge, in the same way, but allowing ^{3}/8-inch seam allowance in total.
3. Cut 19 (24) inches of twill tape and pin ends to wrong side of neck edge, 1^1/4 inches from both ends.
4. Press under a ^{3}/4-inch double hem, as before, on the neck edge and topstitch in place.

5. Cut the remaining twill tape in half and stitch one length to either side of the apron at the waist.
6. Hem the lower edge, allowing a 3/4-inch double hem.
7. Place the pocket pieces together, right sides facing, and stitch around the edges, allowing a 3/8-inch seam and leaving a small opening for turning. Trim corners, clip curves, turn right side out, and press. Slip stitch opening closed.
8. Topstitch pocket in place on front of apron, reinforcing stitching at upper corners.

Tip

If making more than one size, write the name and size onto your pattern pieces and store each size separately in a ziplock plastic bag. When you're ready to make another one, you won't have to wonder which pattern piece is which.

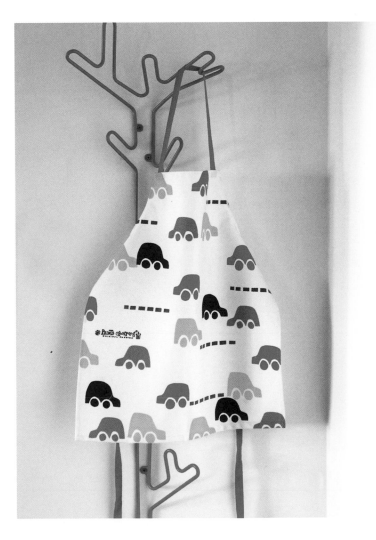

Round tablecloth

Think big scale here and create your own contemporary look. Use bold colors and large motifs for maximum impact. For a round tablecloth, you will need wide fabric, whether you are printing or appliquéing. Use an old, large sheet or buy new cotton sheeting from a good fabric shop. Plain quilt backing also comes in wide sizes and bleached or natural muslin can be found up to 94 inches wide.

Measurements

The cloth can be made to fit any size table.

What you need

- Fabric (see Step 1, page 136)
- Dressmaker's chalk
- Sewing thread

Screen printing

Measure and cut your fabric, following Steps 1 to 3, on page 136. Print the fabric before you hem it, so that you're not printing over "ridges" made by the hem. The Candelabra motif (without the dotted line) can be used at any size for this project or in a combination of sizes. We also used a plain octagon in the design, which we cut by tracing around the dotted line on the motif. Following the instructions under **Step-by-step printing,** on page 24, print your cloth as desired. We printed hexagons randomly first, in the palest color, and then overprinted with positive Candelabra motifs in a variety of sizes. Choose complementary colors and try playing with the scale of the motif. You can print an all-over design, as we have done, or repeat the motif round the hem line.

Not screen printing?

Appliqué big bold shapes or motifs to your background cloth. If you are opting for the frayed edge, you can also leave a raw edge on your appliqué motifs, so that they will fray as well to match the hem line.

What you do

1. Measure the radius of your table top (that is, from center to edge) and add your desired overhang. Add another $3/4$ inch for hems. This is your final measurement: make a note of it.

2. Fold your fabric in half crosswise and then in half again lengthwise. (You are effectively folding it in quarters.)

3. Place your tape measure on the folded corner and measure out your final measurement along one edge and mark with dressmaker's chalk. Do this at 4-inch intervals to form an arc to the other folded edge. Join the marks to make your cutting line. Cut out along this line, through all layers. When you unfold the fabric, you should have a circle.

4. Press under $3/8$ inch on the raw edge, then press under another $3/8$ inch and topstitch or hand-sew the double hem in place. Hemming on the curve can be tricky, so take your time.

5. Alternatively, you could do a double row of stitching $3/8$ inch in from the cut edge and let the washing machine do the work to fray the edge of the tablecloth. You may have to "trim" your tablecloth after washing, as some bits will fray more than others.

Placemats

Canvas and denim are great for placemats, as they have body that will protect your table. Choose some plain canvas for the fabric where your plate will go and some patterned fabrics for the edging. Why not choose fabrics that look great together and make a set that has each placemat "the same, but different?" If printing your own fabric, overprint and make an interesting length so that when you cut it up to make the placemats, they will all be subtly different.

Measurements

Finished mats measure 25 × 14³/4 inches.

What you need

(For 6 placemats)

- ⁷/8 yard × 47-inch plain canvas or denim
- ²/3 yard × 47-inch contrast plain canvas
- 1¹/2 yards × 47-inch plain cotton, for backing
- Sewing thread

Screen printing

We used the detail from the Candelabra motif at actual size for this project. Remove the selvages from the contrast plain fabric and cut it into six 12 × 15¹/2-inch rectangles. Following the instructions under **Step-by-step printing**, on page 24, print each rectangle with a repeated design of the detail from the Candelabra motif, in the color or colors of your choice.

What you do

1. From the plain canvas, cut six 15¹/2-inch squares.

2. Cut each of your printed rectangles in half, giving six pairs of rectangles, each 6 × 15¹/2 inches.

3. With right sides together, and allowing ³/8-inch seams, stitch a printed rectangle to either side of a plain square.

4. Press the seam allowance open and topstitch on each side of the seam, to keep it flat and to help prevent fraying.

5. From backing fabric, cut six rectangles, 25³/4 × 15¹/2 inches.

Tip

For an even sturdier and more heat-resistant mat, you could add a layer of thin cotton quilt batting to the placemats, when you sew on the backing. Trim the seam allowance of the batting close to the seam line to reduce bulk, before turning mats right side out.

Not screen printing?

Use interesting fat quarters or other printed fabrics to make the borders for your placemats. If you make every border different, it's a great way to use up narrow scraps.

6. With right sides together and allowing 3/8-inch seams, stitch a backing rectangle to each placemat around all four edges, leaving an opening in one edge for turning.

7. Trim corners, turn right side out and press.

8. Topstitch around all edges of placemats, about 1/4 inch from the edge, closing the opening at the same time.

Napkins

Another great present idea! Lightweight fabrics are best for napkins, so go through your stash to see what you have and create a wonderful crazy napkin set.

Measurements

We like a generous napkin, about 24 inches square, but you could make it smaller if you like.

What you need

- Two 24-inch squares of fabric (per napkin)
- Sewing machine
- Sewing thread
- Perle cotton No 8, in colors of your choice
- Embroidery needle

What you do

1. Pin the squares together, right sides facing each other.

2. Allowing a $3/8$-inch seam allowance, stitch the squares together around the outer edges, leaving an opening of about 4 inches in one side.

3. Turn the napkin right side out, slip stitch the opening closed, and press well.

4. Using perle cotton No 8, stitch through all layers to embellish, using embroidery stitches as desired (see **Stitch guide**, on page 16). Stitch about $5/8$ inch in from the edge, so that you avoid stitching through all the layers of the seam allowance. This will make the embellishing much easier.

Tip

If you want to make napkins out of a single layer of fabric rather than double, run a line of stitching around the edge of each napkin, about $5/8$ inch from the edge, and fray the edges to the stitching line. How easy is that!

Tea cozy

A good tea cozy is a thing of beauty and adds immeasurably to the whole tea-drinking ritual. But who said the tea cozy had to be knitted? Use leftover quilt batting and scraps of fabric to make a standout cozy for your favorite teapot!

Measurements

14 inches wide × 8$1/2$ inches high, including the frayed edge. Make a paper pattern and fit it over your own teapot — if it doesn't fit, adapt the pattern as necessary.

What you need

- Tracing paper
- One fat quarter in each of two different fabrics
- 23$1/2$-inch square of fabric, for lining
- 23$1/2$-inch square thin quilt batting
- Perle cotton No 8
- Embroidery needle
- Sewing thread

Pattern piece

The pattern piece — tea cozy — is printed on the pattern sheet at the back of the book. Trace the outline onto tracing paper, making sure to trace the cutting line for the batting as well. The pattern piece includes $5/8$-inch seam and hem allowance.

What you do

1. Using your traced pattern, cut one tea cozy shape from each of your fat quarters and two shapes from your lining fabric.

2. Following the batting cutting line, cut two slightly smaller shapes from your batting.

3. Lay a lining piece, right side down, on your work area. Top with batting, and then the fat quarter tea cozy, right side up. Repeat for the remaining pieces. You should have two "sandwiches" of fabric, with batting in between.

4. Allowing a 5/8-inch seam, stitch around the edges so that you enclose the smaller-size batting between the outer layers of fabric.

5. Run some simple lines of machine-quilting (or do it by hand, if you prefer) over the sandwich to keep the batting in place.

6. As the mood takes you, add some embroidered embellishment to your cozy, using embroidery stitches as desired (see the **Stitch guide**, on page 16).

7. Trim the lining fabric back to about 1/8 inch from the seam line.

8. Pin the two quilted pieces together, with the lining sides facing each other, and stitch around the curved edge, following the previous line of stitching.

9. Now fray around the curved edge and trim.

10. Turn under 5/8 inch on lower edge and hem in place.

11. Now take the time to have a cup of tea and admire your work.

Tip

You can create a lovely effect — and use up a few fabric scraps as well — by stitching a few pieces of fabric into a random patchwork, then cutting your tea cozy shapes from the resultant cloth. Don't worry about where the joins occur: make them a feature on your finished cozy by quilting along the seam lines.

Outdoor living

A picnic or a day at the beach never looked so good. Dig into your stash and use all your wonderful stand-out colorful fabrics to brighten up your day out.

Kids' beach shorts

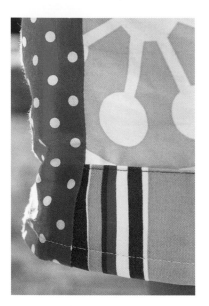

Make crazy patch shorts out of leftover fabrics. Make one leg plain, the other patterned, and then add a pocket for sea shells or stone collecting.

Measurements

To fit a child aged 5-6 (7–8, 9–10) years.

What you need

- Tracing paper
- Two or more contrasting fabrics (since you will be using scraps, make sure you have enough by placing the pattern pieces on your fabrics. You need twice the length of each pattern piece, in total)
- Sewing thread
- 1 inch-wide elastic, to fit around child's waist

Pattern pieces

The pattern pieces for the shorts — front and back — are printed on the pattern sheet at the back of the book in three sizes. 5/8-inch seam allowance and 1¼-inch hems, where appropriate, are included on all pieces. Trace the size you need onto tracing paper.

What you do

1. If you are using a single piece of fabric, fold it in half lengthwise, right sides together, pin the pattern pieces to the wrong side of the double fabric, and cut out. You should cut two fronts and two backs. If you are using different fabrics, lay the pieces on the fabrics and cut them individually, making sure you end up with two fronts and two backs. Each piece in the pair should be a mirror-image of the other.

2. Follow the instructions under **Pajama shorts**, on page 72, to make up your shorts.

Tip

Add a pocket to the front or back of the shorts, if you like. Cut out a rectangle of fabric to the size you think would suit the proportion of the shorts leg. Double hem across the top of the pocket, and then iron the other three sides under. Topstitch the pocket onto the shorts before sewing the front and back together.

Beach bag

Easy to see on a crowded beach, this is a big, bright bag for everything that you need to take to the beach. We used bright, bold colors on a canvas fabric for extra durability. You could piece together leftover canvas, denim, or twill to create a funky patchwork bag. Use large pieces to make the look more contemporary.

Measurements

Finished bag is about 13 × 13 × 14 inches.

What you need

- Tracing paper
- 1²/₃ yards × 47-inch sturdy patterned fabric
- 1¹/₃ yards × 47-inch plain cotton fabric, for lining
- Four 1 inch-diameter metal grommets and grommet tool
- Sewing thread

Template

Following the measurements on the diagram, below, trace a template for your bag on tracing paper. ⁵/₈ inch seam allowance is included in all measurements.

fold line

7³/₄ inches   7³/₄ inches

15¹/₂ inches   15¹/₂ inches

Diagram for beach bag includes ⁵/₈-inch allowance

15¹/₂ inches

What you do

1. Fold your patterned fabric in half crosswise, right sides together, and cut one bag piece, placing the top of your template on the fabric fold. Cut also two straps, each 32 × 6 inches.

2. Fold the lining fabric in half, right sides together, and cut one bag piece.

3. With right sides together, pin the side seams of the outer bag and stitch, allowing 5/8-inch seams. Snip in toward the seam at each inner corner, taking care not to cut the stitching itself. Press under 3/4 inch around the top raw edge.

4. Repeat Step 3 for the lining bag.

5. Turn the outer bag right side out and slip the lining bag inside, wrong sides together, side seams and pressed upper edges matching. Pin the upper edges together.

6. Topstitch all round the upper edge of the bag, and then make another row of topstitching, about 1/4 inch below the first row.

7. Following the manufacturer's instructions, insert a grommet in each upper corner of two opposite sides of the bag, positioning the center of each grommet about 1 1/4 inches down from the upper edge and 1 1/4 inches in from the side seam.

8. To make the straps, fold over and press 1 1/2 inches along one long side of each strap piece. Fold over and press 3/8 inch on the other long side. Now fold this edge over again towards the center and press, so the raw edges are enclosed and the strap is 2 1/2 inches wide. Topstitch close to the inner pressed edge to secure. Now topstitch close to the outer edges. Make another two rows of topstitching between the rows you have already stitched (five rows in all). This will strengthen your handles. Don't worry about the raw ends.

9. Roll the ends of the straps tightly to thread them through the grommets, then unroll them and knot the ends to prevent them pulling bck through.

10. Fill your bag with towels, sunscreen and a good book, and then head to the beach.

Tip

For a waterproof bag, why not cut the lining of your bag from oilcloth? It's easy to sew and comes in a range of wonderfully bright floral prints and geometric patterns.

Umbrella bunting

The scallop edging around this umbrella is easy to make and your umbrella will be a standout on the beach! The finished bunting can also be used for a number of decorative ideas: hang it in the garden as a party decoration, or in a child's room to add color and fun. For a special occasion, why not make enough to go round a marquee?

Measurements

The length of the bunting can be varied to suit whatever you're attaching it to. Each finished scallop is 6 inches wide × 8 inches high.

What you need

- Tracing paper
- Selection of lightweight cotton fabrics in a mix of colors and designs
- Plain fabric, for backing (this doesn't have to be all the same color; use scraps from your stash)
- 1-inch bias binding (20 inches longer than the circumference of your umbrella)
- Beach umbrella
- Sewing thread
- Safety pins (optional)

Pattern piece

The pattern piece for the scallop — Bunting Scallop — is printed on the pattern sheet at the back of the book. Trace onto tracing paper. The traced line will be your sewing line. Remember, when cutting from fabric, to add seam allowance.

What you do

1. Using the pattern piece, trace the required number of Scallops onto your fabrics. We find it easier to cut out pairs of rectangles, right sides together, and then trace the shape onto the wrong side of one of the rectangles.

2. With right sides together, sew the pairs together around the traced edge, leaving the top straight edge open.

3. Trim away the excess fabric in the seam allowance to about $1/4$ inch and clip across the seam allowance on the curve, so that you get a nice smooth line when you turn the scallops right side out. Turn each scallop right side out and press flat with the iron.

4. Lay your bias binding, wrong side up, on a flat surface and position the top edge of the finished scallops on the binding, with the raw edge in the middle of the binding. Arrange the scallops so they abutt directly against one another at the sides, or position them at an equal interval apart.

5. Fold the edge of the binding over, pin to hold, and then stitch through all layers to secure, stitching until you have stitched all the scallops in place.

6. Attach your bunting along each panel edge of the umbrella in one of two ways: either safety pin it from behind (so you don't see the pins) at each panel, or, for a more permanent trim, stitch it in place by hand, along the edge of the umbrella.

Tip

If you're making your bunting to hang across the garden, remember to leave a good length of binding at each end of the bunting, so that you can tie it in place.

Women's sun shirts

Nothing to wear to the beach? No longer a problem after you whip up a few of these. Come to think of it, they're not just for the beach — they're great with jeans to wear anywhere! So grab yourself a couple of oversized cotton shirts and get going. Print on them, appliqué on them, stitch into them, change the buttons on them ...

Measurements

The technique will work on any size shirt.

What you need

- Secondhand shirt (see **Tip**, at left)
- Embellishments, as desired

What you do

This is more about inspiration than actual instruction, so have a look at the details on the shirts that we've made, and then let your imagination get to work. Cut the sleeves and/or the collar off, change the buttons, add bits of ribbon or fabric, embroider, print motifs — just begin and see where it leads you!

Tip

Source your shirts from thrift stores: you'll be surprised by what good quality cotton you can find. Don't forget to check out the men's section as well for great white business shirts. Keep hunting all year so you have them ready for summer.

Sundress

This little dress is easy to make and wear. Throw it over your swimsuit and off you go.

Measurements

To fit a little girl aged 2 (4, 6) years.

What you need

- Tracing paper
- $2/3$ ($3/4$, $7/8$) yard × 44-inch colorful lightweight 100% cotton
- 1 yard × $5/8$-inch contrasting bias binding
- Sewing machine
- Sewing thread

Pattern piece

The pattern piece for the dress — front/back — is printed on the pattern sheet at the back of the book in three sizes. $5/8$-inch seam allowance and $1\frac{1}{4}$-inch hems are included on all pieces. Trace the size you need onto tracing paper.

What you do

1. Fold your fabric in half lengthwise and cut two front/backs (back and front of the dress are the same). For the shoulder tie, cut one 4-inch strip, across the width of the fabric.

2. With right sides together and allowing 5/8-inch seams, stitch front to back at the side seams. Overlock or zigzag the raw edges to finish seams and prevent fraying.

3. Cut a piece of bias binding to fit each armhole, plus a little overlap. Open out one of the folded sides of the bias binding and iron flat.

4. With right sides together, stitch a bias strip to each armhole edge, from the top of front to the back. Press the bias to the wrong side of the dress with your iron and topstitch along the folded edge of the bias to secure. Trim ends of bias even with neck edge of dress.

5. To create the casing for the shoulder tie, fold over and press 3/8 inch to the inside on the raw top edge of the front and back. Press under another 1 inch and topstitch this double hem close to the inner pressed edge.

6. Fold the shoulder tie in half lengthwise, with right sides together. Allowing a 3/8-inch seam, stitch the edges together, stitching across the ends at a 45-degree angle to make points and leaving a small opening in the long edge, for turning. Trim the points, and then turn the tie right side out. Slip stitch opening closed and press well.

7. Thread the tie through the front and back casing, and then finish by tying into a bow at one shoulder.

8. Press under a double hem on the lower edge of the dress and machine-stitch in place.

Picnic blanket

The picnic blanket has never looked so grand! Fun and practical is how we see this project and it's another great one for using up leftover pieces of fabric.

Measurements

Our blanket measures 78 inches square, including the fringe, but obviously, you could make it any size that suits.

What you need

- About 27¹/₂ inches square each of nine different fabrics (see **Tip**, below right)
- 9¹/₄ yards cotton fringe
- Sewing thread

What you do

1. Cut your fabrics into nine 25¹/₂-inch squares. Zigzag or overlock all edges of your squares before you start joining them. (The blanket gets big, so it's much easier to do this first.)

2. Arrange the squares into three rows of three and mix them around until you are happy with the arrangement.

3. Allowing ⁵/₈-inch seams, stitch the squares together as laid out. Press the seams open as you go, and topstitch close to each seam on either side.

4. Trim the edges of the completed blanket with cotton fringe, folding and stitching the corners into miters as you come to them.

Tip

Use denims (pre-wash these to make sure they don't run), twills, and other medium- to heavy-weight fabrics. Go for wow factor and use big motifs and bright colors. Use old tablecloths or gingham: how "picnic happy" can you get!

Acknowledgments

Thank you: ❀ To my three beautiful boys, Baz, Dylan, and Toby ... for always looking after me., and giving me endless hugs and kisses. ❀ Mum, for all the encouragement, love, and sunshine. ❀ And Kirsten, for her passion, enthusiasm, and true, dear friendship ... you make me laugh.
Cath

For your endless support and love, thank you, Steve: you know me better than me. ❀ Pearl, Lucy, and Henry, for just being your wonderful selves. ❀ Mum, for the endless help and true belief in what I do. ❀ And Dad ... who would have thought! ❀ Robyn and Bob, for support always. ❀ Cath, for your friendship and sharing your truly wonderful ideas with me: here's to many a more B and D together ... and laughs and tears ...
Kirsten

We would both like to thank:
❀ Christina Scala and David Studdy and Brio, for letting us take over their beautiful home. ❀ Sally Smith, for sharing her house with us. ❀ Sarah Adams, who has been with us from shed to studio. ❀ Warwick Orme, Michele Cranston, and Mary-Louise Brammer, for their belief. ❀ Our Wednesday night girls: you're all fab! ❀ Jacqui, for keeping all things Prints Charming ticking. ❀ Dylan, Toby, Pearl, Lucy, and Henry, for being such wonderful Prints Charming models. ❀ Our team of sewers, for turning our ideas into reality. ❀ Emi, for her wonderful instinctive quilting: a special thank you. ❀ Alan and Vince, our favorite tea towel couriers. ❀ Zoe Finlay-Jones, thanks so much for all the "coaching." ❀ Marcus Fabrics in NY, for turning our hand-printed artwork into yards of beautiful fabric. ❀ Material Obsession, Patchwork on Central Park, Addicted 2 Fabric, and Ballarat Patchwork: four local fabric shops who were visionaries and sold our first hand-printed fabric range. ❀ Kay Scarlett, for truly making it happen. ❀ Vivien, Sophia, and Katrina, for guiding us through the world of publishing a book, and extending our vocab. ❀ Alex, for her great design. ❀ Georgina, for crossing our t's and dotting our i's: here's to more coffees together. ❀ Patient Julie, for taking such beautiful photos, styled so wonderfully by the tireless and quirky Janine.

To ST, thanks.

Resources

Fabrics, kits, and accessories are available from Prints Charming, www.printscharming.com.au

Matilda's Own "Grandma's Star" templates are available on the net and in quilting stores. See www.victoriantextiles.com.au or visit JT Trading at www.sew-craft.com in the United States.

This book has been written so you don't have to use just Prints Charming fabrics; simply print your own fabrics, or work with a natural base cloth. We have included tips on why we use certain fabrics and what you could use if you can't find the exact thing. For further inspiration on fabrics, visit:

www.bamboofabricstore.com, an eco-friendly store in New Jersey selling bamboo fabric in a variety of weights to print on.

www.fabrics-store.com, a great online store that sells a wonderful range of linens and cottons in an array of colors.

www.hempfabricshop.com sells hemp and other eco-friendly fabrics.

www.homeecshop.com is a store in Los Angeles and a good resource for ideas, fabrics, and haberdashery.

www.jandofabrics.com is a shop in New Jersey that sells a variety of fabrics from denims through to other natural fabrics to print on.

www.jcarolinecreative.com is another great online store that sells a huge range of fabrics and contemporary fabrics and trims.

www.marcusfabrics.com stocks Oasis colored organic cotton, great as a solid or to print on.

www.pearlpaint.com will satisfy you screen printing needs.

www.pinkchalkfabrics.com, great for the contemporary sewer.

www.presenciausa.com can direct you to your local supplier of Finca perle cotton No 8 threads that we use all the time.

www.reprodepot.com sells great solids.

www.spoolsewing.com is a great store in Philadelphia.

Copyright © 2010 by Murdoch Books Pty Limited

All rights reserved.

Published in the United States by Potter Craft, an imprint of the Crown Publishing Group, a division of Random House, Inc., New York. Originally published in Australia as *Prints Charming* by Murdoch Books Pty Limited.

www.crownpublishing.com
wwww.pottercraft.com

POTTER CRAFT and colophon is a registered trademark of Random House, Inc.

Library of Congress Cataloging-in-Publication Data is available upon request

ISBN 978-0-307-58659-9

Printed in China

Design by Alex Frampton
Photography by Julie Renouf
Styling by Janine Moller

10 9 8 7 6 5 4 3 2 1

First American Edition